DUST ON MY SHOULDERS

DUST ON MY SHOULDERS

PETER MARR

Copyright © 2002 by Peter Marr.

Library of Congress Number: 2002091893
ISBN: Hardcover   1-4010-5641-5
       Softcover   1-4010-5640-7

All rights reserved. No part of this book may be reproduced or transmitted in any form or by any means, electronic or mechanical, including photocopying, recording, or by any information storage and retrieval system, without permission in writing from the copyright owner.

This book was printed in the United States of America.

To order additional copies of this book, contact:
Xlibris Corporation
1-888-795-4274
www.Xlibris.com
Orders@Xlibris.com
15135

CONTENTS

INTRODUCTION 9

PREFACE 11

CHINA
    FRONT TAIL OF BULL 16

THE VAIL RANCH
    "PROGRESS" MARCHES ON 26

MEXICO
    DUST ON YOUR SHOULDERS 38

REAL ESTATE 1A
    COLDWELL BANKER AS IT WAS 56

THE DARK CONTINENT
    INTO AFRICA 68

THE ENGLISH
    GOD BLESS THEM 80

THE RANCH
    A PASTORAL CHILDHOOD 100

COSTA RICA
    THE BIG GUY 112

BAJA AND MOTORCYCLES
    THE LAST FRONTIER 120

IRELAND
    I'LL HAVE A GUINNESS 144

KOREA
    FROZEN CHOSEN 156

BUENOS AIRES
    A PLACE TO TANGO 164

EASTERN EUROPE
    COVERT AND BYZANTINE 174

NEW ZEALAND
    DOWNED DOWN UNDER 192

AUTHORS NOTE 207

EPILOGUE
    PATHS CROSSED: MEMORABLE PEOPLE 209

Design:	**The Dalton Press**
Editor:	**Shirley Schieber**
Illustrations:	**Deanne West**
Headlines:	**Shelly Mulcahy**
Counsel:	**Marilyn Tucker-Beesemeyer**

With grateful acknowledgment to all who travel with me and "get dust on their shoulders" on the road of life.

INTRODUCTION

In his first full-length book, *Dust on my Shoulders,* Peter Marr reminisces about his journey through life. Moving from minibooks to a major work, he offers the reader a larger than life look at his odyssey of business, travel and personal experiences.

His writing is crisp and clear, descriptions are detailed photographs caught in the moment and facts and figures are accurately remembered over time.

Subtle but robust, the strength of his style is displayed in this collection of entertaining episodes and animated anecdotes.

A graduate of Claremont McKenna College in California, he is a third generation Californian born in Los Angeles. He spent 38 years at Coldwell Banker, now CB Richard Ellis, where he held 15 different positions including that of founding their International Department.

Peter also served as a Diplomatic Courier for the United States State Department traveling to its embassies in Europe, Africa and the Middle East. Now retired, he lives in Newport Beach, California.

Dust on my Shoulders is a description of Peter's experiences, adventures, friends and associates and reflects a James Thurber approach to an autobiography in short pieces.

Shirley Dalton Schieber

PREFACE

When I began this book, I knew of course that I had been exposed to a monumental number of interesting people. There have been so many, that actually selecting those covered here was so difficult, it may force me to contemplate a sequel.

If I have another book in me, how could I not chronicle **Bill Arce** and **Jess Cone**, my football coaches at Claremont whose direction and counseling so influenced my future life; **John Bayley**, my wonderful Kiwi mate from Auckland;: **Dick Hungate**, my former father-in-law, who at 93, can outrun most 50 year olds; **John Gilchrist**, my first Newport landlord and mentor for years; **Jerry Asher**, the Maestro of the Westside who can always lift my spirits; **Bob McNulty**, that marvelous dot com promoter who always seems to fall on his feet and **Feroze Bundum,** that irrepressible Mauritian/Turk/Englishman who can't do enough for you.

Bill Langston, a Carolina gentleman who has learned to blend business and pleasure better than any man I know; **Nick Frazee,** both a teammate and valued friend whose name and reputation is synonymous with generosity; Bob and Kris Allison, who have so much and give so much; Derek **and Pat Butler,** who have a cameo role in this book but are stars in my life; **Pedro Seabra,** who so nobly saw to my well being in Lisbon; **Agustin Alvarado** in Mexico City, one of CB's best managers and nicest men, and **Larry and Carolyn Nield,** wonderful cow folks from Wyoming who have shown us so dramatically just how much we miss in the city.

Julie Owen who served me faithfully and unselfishly for so many years; **George Butterfield** who cares; **George Kallis,** the raspy voiced CB Exec who never failed me; **Frank Mahoney,** who ran CB so very well with great amounts of heart and compassion; **Wynn Griffith,** a noble former wife and mother of my children; **Ned Marr** and **Amy Doyle, Rory and Lizzie O'Donoghue,** who have the strength to continue the fight with both Mugabe and illness in Zimbabwe; **John Parker,** my old mentor who gave me my first chance in the sun and **Eileen Savdie,** that wonderful liberal Parisian with whom I love to disagree.

Or how about the Judge, **Bruce Sumner,** kind, insightful, intelligent and such a valiant fighter; **Chris Thrift,** a limey in the finest connotation who livens things up anywhere he goes; **Shinichi Kotoya** and **Tatsumi Hanaya,** who made me appreciate Japan, a land that I had already loved; **Luis Donaldson,** a better South American host you could never have, **Evan White,** who always made me nervous as he did his agenda for his Canadian Board Meetings over a bagel five minutes before the board congregated and **Roberto Trella,** that wonderful Roman bon vivant.

How could I forget **Big John Forrester** and his wonderful DTZ soldiers from Throgmorton Street in London; **Richard and Jane Leider,** who brought a bit of San Francisco to Hong Kong; **Philippe Leigniel,** a gracious Frenchman in a country of grace; or **Frank Eul,** that feisty scrappy Englishman whom I never tire of. And how about all my friends, both members and employees, at **Big Canyon** and **Las Cruces,** two of the trinity of my favorite places, the third corner being **CB Richard Ellis** with all of those "dog soldiers and infantrymen."

Lastly, and most importantly, all of my family. You have only had cameo roles in this production, but you could have filled up a bookshelf yourselves. Both my immediate and extended families are world class and represent such a huge part of my life. Thanks for your support and love. It is reciprocated.

China

"We touched down in Beijing after midnight on a cold November evening in a near empty 747. We were ushered through the vacant Beijing Airport, whose gloomy interior was painted puke-green and smelled of disinfectant"

CHINA

FRONT TAIL OF BULL

It was 1992 and I had just assumed the responsibility of heading up an international operation for Coldwell Banker Commercial, one of America's major real estate service companies. Its goal was to expand its real estate services capabilities across the world. As a company, we were internationally incompetent. At that time, the company's meager international business featured our "flagship", a joint venture Canadian operation in which the respective C.E.O.s couldn't abide each other. Secondly, they had a smart young Spanish speaking "cowboy" based in San Diego who was forging hordes of big Tijuana warehouse deals with Asian companies looking for a tax-free conduit for their products in the states. Lastly, CB had three people occupying hugely expensive space in Berkeley Square in London. The success of this group was preordained, as it had been permanently hog-tied by incongruously refusing to accept fees for its services thus becoming incapable of generating any income. A combination of expensive quarters and no income is usually short term. It was. In other words, International was not something that our people spent much time thinking or bragging about. But our clients were thinking and operating internationally and CB couldn't afford to be left at the altar. So the education of Peter Marr as an Internationalist was appropriate and timely.

In 1992, the Coldwell Banker Commercial International Department was a single under-paid attorney (at least he told anyone who would listen to him that he was underpaid) who the chairman had charged with finding and establishing an alliance with an international property company. When I first became involved with International, Greg, albeit very well meaning, was butchering a potential relationship with a fine British based company, who were great prospects for a European alliance partner. Greg was a wonderful attorney who thought he was a superb negotiator. He wasn't. Thus, my first international chore became keeping Greg off the front lines and allowing him to create ideas and documentation behind the scenes instead of dealing with people. In this we were both ultimately successful.

In the middle of these European talks, I had a call from Rob Aigner who ran the Seattle office for Coldwell Banker Commercial. His office was working with some Chinese buyers who had exceptionally close ties with the People's Republic of China. Their Ministry of Construction had a real estate problem in Beijing, yet undefined, and if we would make ourselves available there, the Chinese would cover our expenses.

This exposure seemed a logical step towards the "internationalization" of Peter Marr. I was excited to make my maiden voyage to China and see firsthand this emerging powerhouse. A delegation was put together which was led by me and included Rob, two of his salesmen, the client's point man and a Mr. X from Hong Kong. We never did find out where Mr. X fit, but knew he had to be a piece of the puzzle. He was fluent in Mandarin, Cantonese and reasonably so in English and had traveled extensively in the People's Republic, so we were willing to accept his mysterious demeanor.

We touched down in Beijing after midnight on a cold November evening in a near empty Northwest Boeing 747. We were ushered through the vacant Beijing Airport, whose gloomy interior was painted puke green and smelled of disinfectant. The baggage carousel must have been designed by Rube Goldberg and squeaked and rattled as it made its endless circles. The whole aura was third world.

There is little doubt that the Chinese manual on business etiquette says, "greet your guests at the airport." To greet this terribly late flight, there were a half a dozen minor luminaries who had driven some thirty miles from the city center for a five-minute appearance. As the plane was five hours late, God knows how long they had suffered this depressing structure. They greeted us, shook hands and left, their governmental responsibility having been met.

The airport was connected to the city by a state-of-the-art toll road that had been built in hopes of convincing the International Olympic Committee that China should host the 2000 Olympics. While their efforts weren't successful in the short term (Sydney was awarded the 2000 Games), Beijing has since prevailed and will host the 2008 games. It does seem to me that the Olympics have become extremely expensive to host. Take the post nine eleven demands for security and add the additional smudge of Salt Lake's payola, and perhaps cities will cease to salivate for the honor of staging the games.

Our drive into the city was almost ethereal. Leaving the toll-way we headed south to Chang-Ya, the huge boulevard that bisects Beijing from east to west. It has twelve lanes of traffic but was virtually deserted during these early hours of the morning. Never again were we to see China without crowds. Little did we know what a treat it was to glide past Tiananmen Square, the Palace of Culture and the Imperial Palace all void of traffic and inhabitants other than a smattering of ever-present night people. That soft evening's drive has left a permanent impression upon my mind; one that Alzheimer's might even have difficulty eradicating.

The next morning we commenced a series of meetings with governmental agencies and government controlled construction companies. It became clear that these men (few women were present other than in fairly menial jobs) were achievers. Under the Chinese communist system all people were paid somewhat similar wages. But "the movers and the shakers" made up for their modest stipend they received from additional perks. These men had big homes, their own cars and drivers, lavish expense accounts and even personal cooks. The chefs were considered a major perk as they were usually recruited or stolen from other agencies or private restaurants. They were treated like royalty by their masters and were famous for preparing China's finest, most creative dishes, which made their employers appear prestigious in front of their peers and clients.

Now as senior member of this Lilliputian delegation, I was expected to officially respond to all the platitudes mouthed by the opposite side. The six of us Westerners all sat in a row on one side of an endless table while the Chinese and their interpreters faced us. Protocol called for their making a totally innocuous statement followed by my equally insipid reply. I was expected to comment on how pleasant it was to be there, how impressed we were with the city (never mentioning that we were freezing our asses off and choking on the coal dust) and how hopefully, meetings like this would lead to opportunities between our two cultures. There wasn't much more I could say for none of us had the remotest clue why they were paying for this trip and why the trip was anything other than a boondoggle. Frivolity had no place in these meetings. My counterpart at one of these sessions with the Beijing Development Company was a Mr. Ma. After all the remarks and the responses to the remarks, I mentioned the similarities between our two names, Marr and Ma. I added: "Funny, you don't look Irish". Hopefully, it went over his head.

The best day of the trip was the obligatory visit to the Great Wall and the Imperial Palace. The Chinese always saved a day for every official delegation to see these magnificent sites. Not only is the Great Wall spectacular, but I'm sure our hosts felt that it reassured their guests of the brilliance, foresight and sensitivity of all Chinese. Experiencing these sights first hand leaves you with a very special impression of the culture that could accomplish this so long ago.

PETER MARR

After the Great Wall, we were taken to the Ming Tombs followed with lunch at the government cafeteria on the Ming grounds. We were late, and a few minutes after being seated the lights suddenly were drastically dimmed, all the employees left and we sat in the dark with a barely touched lunch. The cafeteria was state operated and as we were to learn, the "Red Book" said, close at 3PM. The government attitude seemed to say "the customer be damned!" As a footnote, service and response in the privately run restaurants in Beijing was first-rate.

DAXING COUNTY

Near the end of our trip, we finally learned what the Chinese wanted from us. For the first several days there had been no clue from our hosts as to why we had been asked to their spellbinding land. Did they want to expand their real estate appetite in the states? Was this an exploratory move to buy our company? Did they have property problems here they needed help on from America? Each evening, after our diligent guides and escorts departed, we would speculate just what they wanted. None of us were even close.

The first hint was the appearance on our agenda of a visit to Daxing, a city about 20 miles south of Beijing. We were driven into the countryside outside this town of 50,000 where we crept down quiet lanes, crisscrossed canals and scattered the fat white ducks found on the roads bisecting an endless number of small hamlets. The abundance of arable flat land was continually pointed out to us but it didn't take a guide's instruction to recognize that. We then proceeded back to Daxing, down a main street that was as empty as Chang-Ya Boulevard had been on the night we arrived in Beijing. At the north end of Daxing's main street was a modest county building where we were immediately offered tea and ensconced in a seedy second story conference room.

From our vantage point we could see outside and watched as numerous individuals arrived in cars bearing Lexus and Mercedes-Benz insignias.

We were later told that most had been stolen in Southern California, driven across the border at Tijuana and then shipped into China. Some of the passengers were dressed in Mao-like quilted coats and most had the appearance of farmers. They turned out to be county officials and by the looks of their cars, they had a good thing going in Daxing. After the de rigueur round of pre-ordained pap-like introductions, their presentation began.

They wanted us to deliver a DISNEYLAND to Daxing County!

Frankly, we were momentarily speechless. Their intention was admirable, but it was surprising that anybody as bright and entrepreneurial as the Chinese would reach out as blindly as they had by asking us to deliver Disney to the rice paddies of North China. This was not just a naïve little county government making such an improbable request but a unit sponsored by the huge Ministry of Construction. In retrospect, I think it was nothing more than the awkwardness a society faces in dealing with something strange. These particular Chinese simply didn't know how to correctly access the American business machine. They ended up sponsoring our disparate group, as they just didn't know the right Americans to talk to. While China has vast numbers of savvy internationalists, these boys weren't in that club. The Japanese never would have made such a mistake. They would have compiled endless reams of research to assure themselves that they were talking to the right people. Their quest finally made it clear why the mysterious and remote Mr. X had joined us. He was the biggest dreamer of all, for he envisaged himself as the developer for any project that came from this. The cold hard truth is that everyone around the world woos Disney but Disney calls their own shots. After all, over the last 50 years, they have only built four Disneylands!

By this time, we had learned how the game was played. We nodded, said what a fine site it was and most importantly, promised to get their development interests to the attention of the Disney organization. Upon our return we did call Disney and they politely put Daxing somewhere among the scores of requests for a new Disneyland that Disney annually receives. In essence they said; don't call us, we'll call you!

Now in spite of the automotive extravagance shown earlier, Daxing County wasn't flush enough to afford their very own chef, so we proceeded to a downtown restaurant for our "celebration dinner". The workday had finished and the formerly empty cavernous downtown was now jammed with people, push carts, vegetable stalls, clothing kiosks and China's answer to carnival hawkers selling goods looped around sticks while packing their inventory on their back. This was the area's private market, and I have never witnessed such a total antipode. Daxing transformed from a ghost town to Times Square on New Year's Eve within a couple of hours. It gave a little hint of just where communism had broken down— right with the basics, food and clothing, the merchandise offered by most of the kiosks.

Dinner was memorable. It was as if the Chinese were trying to make a point that we were on their playing field and we best follow their rules. They ordered dinner, and it would have been a breach of protocol had we not eaten what was placed in front of us. We did our best to comply, but it was an effort.

As the senior member, I knew that I had to show willingness to at least try everything placed in front of us. The dishes came on endlessly. First was Shark's Fin soup, and then ducks' feet followed by the ducks' webs. A plethora or more standard fare followed one at a time but then came the python strips. Next was deep-fried scorpion (with the stinger poised and hopefully devenomized) that really wasn't as bad as it sounded. But front tail of bull was! It took all my will and determination to force it down without gagging. We finished everything offered, but nobody asked for seconds! Oh, the gastronomical sacrifices we had to make for the good 'ol U.S. of A.!

Back in Beijing, we learned there was one little "catch" about this free trip that we hadn't been appraised of. Supposedly, old Chinese custom say; you treat everybody to dinner the last night. Well they take it literally. We must have had 60 plus people at one of Beijing's finest restaurants for a multi-course meal. The bosses had brought their lieutenants, secretaries, chauffeurs and clerks—all were included. Dinner included endless raised glasses toasting "gambai" using gallons of Chinese firewater while scores of karaoke songs were sung that we never heard before or since. While I got stuck with a big bill, it undoubtedly was the best evening of our stay. Everyone was relaxed and oozed fellowship and to my everlasting relief, my instructions to the restaurant staff that specified that snake and front tail of bull not appear on the table, had been followed!

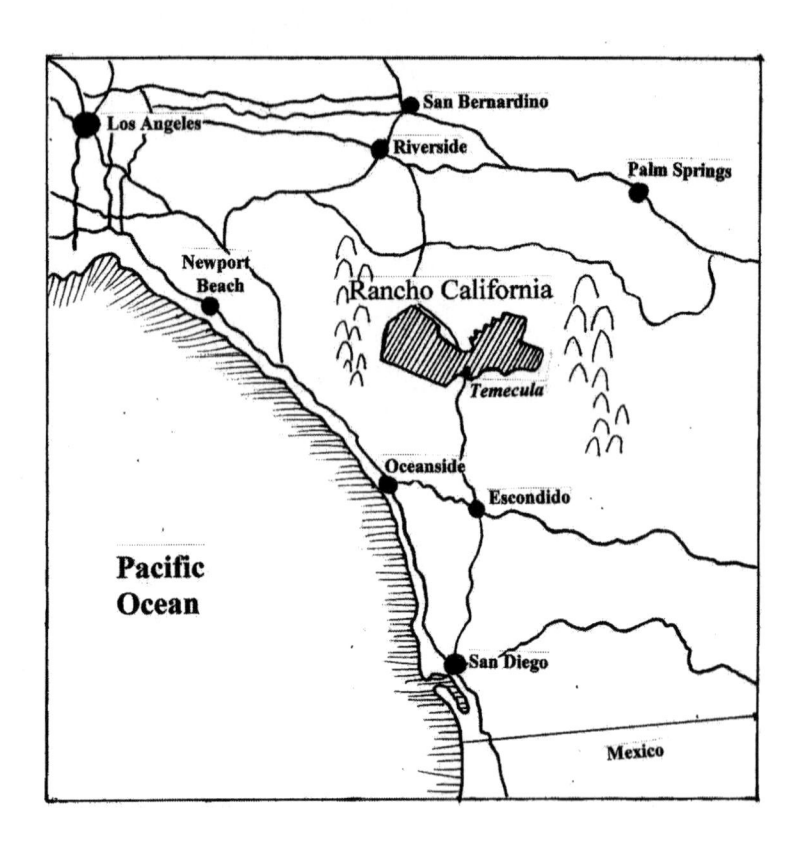

VAIL RANCH

"The patriarch of the Vail Family was a crusty old soul, Mahlon Vail, who loved cattle, land and whiskey probably in reverse order"

THE VAIL RANCH

"PROGRESS" MARCHES ON

The Vail Ranch was an 87,500-acre cattle ranch 70 miles southeast of downtown Los Angeles. It was 35 miles long and 3 to 10 miles wide, almost 135 square miles. The ranch was located in southern Riverside County abutting the San Diego County line and was shaped like a butterfly with the little historic hamlet of Temecula, a former stop on the Butterfield Stage Line located in the body of the insect. The Pauba Ranch, the eastern 45,000 acre wing was a former Spanish land grant. It consisted of some flat valley land with deep alluvial soil surrounded by rolling mesquite and shrub covered hills habituated by dove, coyote, an occasional bobcat and more than an occasional rattlesnake. It also contained an impressive 700-acre body of water, the Vail Lake, complete with the largest private concrete dam in the state.

To the west, in the rocky highlands above Temecula, was a separate land grant, the Santa Rosa Ranch, with its marvelous stands of oak and sycamore. While agriculturally inferior to the eastern land, the Santa Rosa was almost a time warp, an unchanged California portrait from the days of Junipero Serra and the Butterfield Stage Coach. The Vail Ranch could handle about 3000 head of cattle in a good year. The cattle were acquired in the winter, grazed in the luxuriant grasslands through the spring, fattened in feed lots in the lower valleys in the summer and sold for slaughter when the owners guessed the price was right.

The Vail family had been cattle people during two centuries. They had accumulated properties in several locales, including the majority of Santa Rosa Island, one of the larger Channel Islands off the coast of Santa Barbara. The patriarch of the family was a crusty old soul, Mahlon Vail, who loved cattle, land and whisky probably in their reverse order. The family once owned a property called Vail Field, a pioneer landing strip, in what is today the City of Commerce, now one of the premier industrial areas of Los Angeles. Mahlon used to like to say, "You know young man, when they built Los Angeles, they fucked up a mighty fine cattle ranch."

In 1963, Mahlon saw the handwriting on the wall. The Southern California sprawl was getting closer, cattle prices were abysmal and he was in his eighties. He sold the ranch to a joint venture of three real estate companies (including units from the mammoth Kaiser group) for $21,000,000 with the stipulation he be given a life estate to his cabin and grounds in a shaded and secluded oak glen near the shores of Vail Lake. It was a bargain for the new owners. Mahlon Vail only outlived the sale by two years.

While the new ownership of the ranch had capitalization that would have exceeded that of many small countries, they had scrimped on working capital and expected the investment to stand on its own. Obviously, if the land was to become resalable at higher prices, money had to be spent for infrastructure—most notably water and roads, lot splits, planning, marketing, promotion and a staff to develop it. While they still let foreman Louis Rohrpaugh run cattle to keep the property in use, the cattle operation lost money more years than it made it. To generate revenue, they had to sell assets, and their only asset was land.

The joint venture hired my employer, Coldwell Banker, to market the

PETER MARR

property and, shortly after that, retained Bob Unger, the city manager from Costa Mesa, California, to run it. Bob was the manager in Costa Mesa during the time span when it grew from a sleepy little afterthought to its prestigious neighbor, Newport Beach, into one of the more dynamic cities in California. Among other projects, Costa Mesa was home to innumerable influential corporations and to South Coast Plaza, which was to become the largest shopping center in the state. Unger, a nice man with an ego problem, made it clear that he was responsible for the city's success. As it turned out, Bob was more bull shit than substance, and while being effective with the governmental agencies, he had few clues beyond that. With the joint venture demanding a quick turnover to establish a positive cash flow, the result was less than an ideal development process.

In spite of its shortcomings, the project did develop or expand the talents of a tremendous number of notable real estate names in California. The brilliant Jim Knapp was the project's attorney and Lee Sammis, later to become a nationally known developer, parlayed his experience in representing the Irvine Industrial Park into the biggest sale ever consummated on Rancho California. John Parker, Tony French, John O'Donnell, Dick Clotfelter and many others reached great heights in their later careers. They even showed some creative genius in getting there!

Undercapitalized real estate ventures are generally doomed unless they get very lucky or can sell their product very quickly. The developer has to take short cuts to stay afloat and these soon begin to negatively affect the project. This spiral began on the ranch as decisions were based on immediate needs rather than long-term goals. As an example, Unger decided that there was both need and demand for dairy farms, so he developed several hundred acres of land for that purpose. He guessed wrong as only two dairies relocated on the project from the Los Angeles-Orange County market. But the die was cast. Instead of isolating such an undesirable land use, he placed the dairies directly adjacent to proposed retail and residential development. Time has overwhelmed the dairies;

they are gone, replaced by tract houses that were built on enough excrement to keep their lawns green for years to come.

In comparison, the Irvine Ranch in Orange County, a similar sized property, was never undercapitalized. The Irvine ownership was willing and able to spend money that would give them excellent results in the future. A good example of this was the donation of 1000 acres to the University of California for a new university campus. Today the University of California at Irvine has 30,000 students and their influence has been a principal reason that the Irvine Company has been able to attract clean industry to their adjacent properties. While many might have considered the Irvines arrogant, very few will quibble with the final results they realized, and the development of the Irvine Ranch is considered one of the finest examples of planning and implementation in the world.

On the other hand, the Vail Ranch, though far from a disaster, is an example of shortcut planning. First the new ownership came up with a new name. Rancho California was chosen. It was an overly pretentious name and totally lacked any geographical relevance. Forty years later, in spite of great hoopla for the Rancho California project, the name has virtually disappeared and the area has reverted to its former identification, Temecula. No shining light of a name itself, it is at least real and historical. For the record, Temecula is pronounced "Teh MEK yew la" and not "Tem meh KOO la".

In 1963, Rancho California was still rather distant from Southern California's burgeoning expansion and the owners didn't have time to wait for growth to reach it. They did own, however, a dramatic and giant piece of fertile under-developed agricultural land. The ranch still ran cattle, housed its cowboys in bunkhouses and served three meals a day in their mess hall. We often ate lunch (sometimes with prospects in tow,) and I still wonder just what these throwbacks to another era thought of us city slickers in our 4-wheel drive jeeps trying so hard to look like we belonged there.

With no immediate outside growth in sight, the owners sensibly decided to transform grazing land (which needed no improvements other than random fencing) into more sophisticated agricultural land. At the time, cattle land was valued at less than $100 an acre, while prime orchard and crop land could bring as much as $2000 an acre.

Countless studies were commissioned on soil quality, available water and average temperatures to ascertain higher and better farming uses. There turned out to be a number of higher value potential agricultural uses among them: citrus, avocados, row crops and wine grapes to mention a few. All of these needed water to grow. The Metropolitan Water District or M.W.D. managed and provided most of Southern California's water with its two greatest sources being the Colorado River and the Northern California water from the California Aqueduct. But this water was still 20 miles away from the ranch so they set out drilling for water, hoping to find big underground aquifers beneath the ranch. Big water drilling rigs appeared with their drillers nervously watching every move of the water witch manipulating the quivering stick. Southern California Edison Company furnished the witch at no cost. He must have been good, for the wells which were sunk 2000-2500 feet below the ground, produced over 2500 gallons a minute each, a lot of water. They had reached a deep aquifer loaded with water but it would be a "mining operation", as it would take centuries to replenish itself. With outside water in the offing, the Ag boom was off and running.

A typical Coldwell Banker type thought agriculture was the province of guys with a piece of straw between their teeth or some crazy from University of California Davis trying to grow square tomatoes. Shallow thinking on our part when it was pretty well known that agriculture was the state's largest industry. So we hired Richard Dick (forever to be known as Double Dick) from Ralston Purina as our Ag expert. Well, we got more than an Ag expert when we got Richard. He was half snake-oil salesman and half dreamer and had more ideas than the Rand Corporation. While he was no one man team, in the next two years, our little group ended up selling the better part of 10,000 acres for new agricultural use. The buyers ran the gamut from Atlantic Richfield Oil for citrus, Ely Calloway and

Brookside Winery for varietal grapes, Senator John Murdy for row crop land and Liz Whitney Tippett from Lexington, Kentucky for a thoroughbred horse ranch. No pinstripe suits for us, and we cruised the empty country in jeeps and pick-ups wearing Levis and cowboy shirts doing our best to break up a magnificent ranch. We even occasionally could be seen sucking on a piece of straw between our teeth.

My most ignominious personal defeat however was trying to sell property to Rex Ellsworth, the horse breeder who owned the famous thoroughbred, Swaps. Propitiously I had ended our tour on a mesa above the beautiful valley he was considering. He stepped ahead of me to the edge of the bluff and gazed at the scenery. From behind, so not to upset the magic of the moment, I softly said to him, "It's a gorgeous property isn't it, Mr. Ellsworth", and discretely sidled up next to him. I discovered he really wasn't that impressed, merely taking a leak!

THE REAGAN DEAL

Coldwell Banker's chairman, Dick Mott, was as equally crusty a man as was old Mahlon Vail. The two of them got along famously and had many a belt of "Old Yellowtail" together. Like Vail, Mott was a visionary and during his career laid the cornerstone that turned Coldwell Banker into one of the nations most successful real estate behemoths. The Rancho California listing was the biggest the company had, but not many of our people knew or understood it. The sellers had made available their Aero Commander and Jet Ranger helicopter to use for bringing clients to the property and they had done some promotion, but most of all, we had to persuade our internal sales force to experience the ranch first hand in order to appreciate its beauty, grandeur and potential. So Dick Mott agreed that we would have the biggest company picnic in the history of the firm at Rancho California. He asked me to write the notification to our employees and with a grain or two of self-interest, I drafted a memo that suggested they would lose their birthright, commissions and manhood if they didn't attend. Mott did tone it down a bit, but still we had buses, planes, cars and motorcycles arrive from throughout the state that

PETER MARR

Saturday. We arranged donkey races, motorcycle relay races (no fatalities, thank God) and provided all the beer Anheuser Busch could produce in a weekend. It got real wet out there and grown men were dumped into horse troughs filled with ice, audacious wrestling matches took place and Ron Wheatcroft from San Diego played Marlon Brando and rode his Harley inside the Long Branch Saloon in Temecula (with Chairman Mott as a passenger) to cap off the festivities. It was quite a day and did it pay off!

Within a week, I had a call from Al Sparlis who had presented the ranch to the California governor, Ronald Reagan. Al has to be one of the great personalities I have ever known. He had flown in both World War II and Korea and spent time in Vietnam during that conflict. Al had been an All American football player at UCLA and played for Curly Lambeau and the Green Bay Packers where even he had difficulty tackling Bronco Nagurski in practice. Al was a raconteur who could tell jokes for hours and had the appearance and demeanor of a rough-hewn Anthony Quinn. He sold real estate successfully, not necessarily through his knowledge, but through his overwhelming strength of personality and total persistence.

Reagan had sold his former ranch in Malibu Canyon and needed a replacement property. Reagan's modus operandi was the same in his personal life as it became during his terms as president of the United States. He put great faith and trust in those around him. In this case, he had several close friends and associates who agreed to buy all the acreage encircling his holdings in order to protect Reagan from potentially "unsavory neighbors". These friends included Taft Schriber, the president of Music Corporation of America, Bob Reynolds, owner of the California Angel baseball team, Bob Wilson, Reagan's closest friend who later became the U.S. Ambassador to the Vatican and William French Smith, a prominent Los Angeles lawyer.

The parcel Governor Reagan ultimately bought was in the most remote corner of the western property, the Santa Rosa Ranch and accessible only by dirt roads. It was drop-dead beautiful. Groves of ancient oaks, small ponds and sylvan meadows surrounded by sage brushed hills, it truly had to be the epitome of old California.

Since the owners were cutting a piece from a loosely described former Spanish land grant, they had to survey and write a new legal description. Property lines were established that would not allow subsequent buyers of adjoining properties to look into Reagan's valley (yes, the governor was able to call the shots) and as a result, the boundaries ran through hills of chaparral that were virtually inaccessible by foot or horseback. But we still had to mark the property so Reagan could see what he was buying. Lupe Amaya, the seller's helicopter pilot, and I came up with a method to do this. The day before the inspection, we loaded the back of the Jet Ranger with forty-pound sacks of lime. Lupe flew, a surveyor sat co-pilot and I stood inside the open door, attached to the chopper by a safety line. When we located a property corner, I dropped a bag of lime on the site. It was a great success. The following day the governor was able to aerially tour his 1600 acres in less than ten minutes.

Personally, Reagan was a very agreeable and considerate man. He asked me to guide him in a walk through the best parts of his property and when finished, saw to it that we did a tick search on each other's Levis. He said this being cattle country, ticks often brush off the cows, attach to the chaparral and ultimately cling to our clothing. It was nice to learn something practical from a future president. But the future president never used the property. Several years later, he sold it for an enormous profit and used the proceeds to acquire the ranch in Santa Barbara County that ultimately served as his Summer White House.

The day the sale closed, like heat-seeking missiles, the press came to Temecula. We had been warned that the Reagans, and especially Nancy, coveted their personal privacy and we should be circumspect in what we said to the press. I certainly respected this. I was asked to talk to the CBS affiliate station in Los Angeles and gave them a terribly innocuous description of the purchase divulging little more than where it was (a matter of public record) and that the Reagans had been down twice to see it, hopefully indicating that they were caring buyers rather than ciphers. The interview was picked up (it must have been my smile and charm) and shown nationally.

Monday morning, I received a phone call from attorney William French Smith, a most patrician partner of Gibson, Dunn and Crutcher, Los Angeles' premier law firm. He later became Reagan's Attorney General. I knew him well as we had spent a great deal of time working out the details of the sale and I respected him as a fair and obliging man. Bill said, "Peter, Nancy saw your interview over the weekend and I am obliged to tell you that Nancy is upset and feels you should be chastised". He continued, "I saw the interview as well and actually feel you handled it very well, but Nancy can be a real bitch at times!" Now that was memorable. It was a chewing out that left you feeling good.

A footnote on salesman Al Sparlis. Early in the Reagan negotiations, Al was called up by the Air Force to ferry planes to Viet Nam. The Reagan transaction was well under way and I personally substituted for him during his absence. Ultimately, he received a pretty good commission check for the transaction. Most salespeople would say thanks for the help and good-by since I was salaried and couldn't accept commissions. Not Al. He called Wynn, my first wife, and said he knew we were going skiing in Aspen and heard we were short on ski gear. He insisted that we meet him at Kerr's Sporting Goods in Beverly Hills where he proceeded to outfit the two of us in ski gear well beyond our skiing prowess. When he had previously mentioned his intent to outfit us, I had said I couldn't accept his gift. His response was "Get your ass over here so you can at least make the selection. Otherwise I will make the selection myself and leave it on your doorstep". Gruff, tough with the ultimate heart of gold—that was Al.

Since those days, the ranch has ceased to be identifiable as a unit, and if you say Rancho California, people will look at you quite questioningly. The ownership has changed several times. I believe the California Conservancy acquired 10,000 acres of the prettiest property on the Santa Rosa Ranch, which will assure that it remains pristine in perpetuity, a most fortunate happenstance. Temecula is a city with a regional shopping center, the Pechanga Indian gambling casino, numerous golf courses, miles of tract houses (as well as some upscale and palatial horse ranches) and a substantial industrial and office park. It's just not very crisp. Its lack of detailed planning is showing but I am probably being overly critical. I am sure, that most of the people who live there find it a good place to live. All's the pity. With an implementation of planning and an eye for its beauty, it could have easily been more.

MEXICO

"Dionisio Senior especially liked to wander through Garibaldi Square, where the mariachi bands congregated, and he would get several of the bands competing with each other while we drank plastic cupfuls of cheap tequila"

MEXICO

DUST ON YOUR SHOULDERS

On a shelf above my desk stands a simple little sign. It states, ***Once the dust of Mexico has settled on your shoulders, you can never shake it off.***

That pretty much says it all about Mexico.

> It has some very mean poverty, despicable garbage dumps on the edge of every town, unbelievably suicidal drivers, ugly urban sprawl and such a macho society that sometimes it seems to be in danger of devouring itself.
>
> On the contrary, Mexico possesses areas of great natural beauty, some of the most charming and interesting cities on the globe, a deep and revered heritage and most importantly, a high-spirited and hard working people.

LA FAMILIA SANCHEZ

The Sanchez family is part of Mexico's elite. Its circle of friends generally includes the President and most of the business leaders of Mexico City. They build office buildings, retail centers and homes as well as brokering and managing them. Their home is in Los Bosques, which translates to "the woods" and is an apt description of this exclusive forested hillside location in the southern part of the city. Los Bosques has a security system that is tighter than the "The West Wing".

The Sanchez's are something akin to the American dream manifesting itself in Mexico. They have accumulated substantial wealth while ascending from proverbial "humble beginnings". They have done this by being smarter, more creative and more daring than their competition. They have also prospered in spite of their skin color. In Mexico (obviously not alone in the western world) the amount of white pigmentation in one's skin pretty much determines one's social status. The Sanchez's look like Mexicans—not Castilians—and are proud of the stream of Aztec blood that runs through their veins. Even in the most chic of Mexico City's society, they would appear to be accepted wherever they go.

The patriarch of the Sanchez clan is Dionisio Sanchez Gonzalez, a friendly outgoing exuberant man whose enthusiasm infects all those he surrounds. He is average sized with an open face, a perpetual twinkle and giant smile. His English is limited (typically for non-English speakers, he fathoms more than he speaks) but no one has trouble understanding Dionisio. Dionisio and Marta have three children, Dionisio Sanchez Carbajal (with Hispanics, middle names usually come from the mother and appear last) Marta and Arturo. Obviously they had run out of parent's names by the time Arturo made his debut. The brothers now run the business. Daughter Marta need not be involved—she has to be one of the most gorgeous women in Mexico. *Qué lástima*, her very successful husband, Memo, takes excellent care of her.

The first son, Dionisio Sanchez Carbajal is smallish, good looking, conservative and extremely bright. As the oldest son, he has assumed the reins of leadership for the family business. Arturo, the youngest, is showy and gregarious, a gourmand who tends to weight—I know the feeling. He also, is very bright. His *corbatas* were so wild you could pick him out across a room just by his neckwear. Both boys were partially educated in the states thus are almost as much at home in the American culture as they are in Mexico.

My company, CB Commercial, had charged me with identifying and negotiating a commercial real estate brokerage venture with a successful, ethical and forward thinking Mexican firm, one which could see the benefits of a formal relationship with a top American company. After numerous trips, investigations and interviews, we learned that few firms met any of the qualifications and only Grupo SARE, the Sanchez conglomerate, possessed all three.

Again, I had been assigned Greg Spinner, the young, extremely bright attorney who had quite a bit of experience in international law. Sadly, his people skills hadn't improved and never matched his cerebral talent. He must have been a major source for lawyer jokes. Greg did much of the preliminary research as well as some initial negotiations. When left to his own devices, his need to count every bean and cover every potential eventuality, led to desultory negotiations and well meaning but frustrated potential Mexican partners screaming like mariachis who had been stiffed on their tip.

Fortuitously, Greg and I worked pretty well together. The same set of circumstances had taken place in London and was to take place again in negotiations in Hong Kong. Unwittingly, Greg would get the other side's frustration level up to 212° at which time I would step in, be a good guy, give up a little and end up with a strong sustaining relationship. But the Mexicans didn't neglect Greg. When the deal was finished, they took him out on the town, got him smashed beyond belief, and, in the early hours, left him. He didn't find his hotel room until the following morning and even then, I doubt that he knew he was there.

The Sanchez family is not without a touch of arrogance. Perhaps hauteur is synonymous with the wealthy but I think not. The Sanchez's expected things to be done for them, to be served, to be catered to. Many of the nouveau riche (proudly, they were charter members of that group) are sheepish about their new gains and treat their servants like their best friends. Not the Sanchezes. They were never mean spirited and were certainly generous to a fault, but servants, however cherished, were treated like servants. The Sanchez flamboyance was legend. It was not a self-serving pretentious type of conduct, but flashiness is a wonderful Mexican trait. It is part of the culture. Look at their "low riders", listen to their ranchero music, admire the palette of colors used on the exterior of their homes and enjoy the garish aura of their fiestas and you can understand: they love a parade.

Perhaps part of this attitude spilled over to their relationship with Tom Boyd. Tom, a Texan who had found himself in San Diego flying Navy fighters, had become a CB manager there. He just happened to speak fluent Spanish. He was intrigued with the opportunities in the burgeoning Mexico City office and, with the approval of both Mexican and American partners, committed to becoming the first manager of that office. Like other American corporations operating abroad, executives receive a pay package that is generally in excess of what they would have received at home. Tom was no exception, but with the Sanchez's being the majority partner, they of course, paid the majority of the compensation, far more than they were paying their locals. This grated on them and their reaction was to become more and more demanding of Tom, often unrealistically so. They wanted a combination of Superman, George Soros and Harrison Ford and they got "good old Tom". He was plenty good but not good enough for them. They literally drove Tom out of the country with their intransigence, a maneuver that truly tested the partnership to its core. Only their hiring of an outstanding talent, Agustin Alvarado, as Tom's replacement saved the venture. In a happy footnote, Tom returned to Houston where he worked the huge number of multi-national corporations investing in maquiladora sites along the Texas/Mexico border. He became very successful, secretly thumbing his nose at the Sanchezes in the meantime.

Drinking was something the Sanchezes liked to do, and in Mexico, singing goes hand in glove with drinking. When in Mexico City we had to eat where we could drink tequila and sing mariachi tunes such as Coo-ca-roo-coo-coo (the sound made by a dove) and El Rey "The King", which is the informal anthem of machismo. One of their associates, the animated and delightful, Luis Mendez, was an accomplished mariachi singer. Fortunately, he took no umbrage when we gringos would try to shout out a semblance of the words through our self-inflicted mists of Sauza, Herradura or Patron. These demonstrations happened in good restaurants, bad cafes, marketplaces, and even poling through the floating gardens of Xochimilco while tied up to flat bottom boats filled with mariachis.

Dionisio Senior especially liked to wander through Mexico City's Garibaldi Square, where the mariachi bands congregated, and he would get several of the bands competing with each other while we drank plastic cupfuls of cheap tequila purchased from vendors fitted with a tank on their back and a spout in their hand. On one occasion, we were weekend visitors in Valle de Bravo, a popular retreat for wealthy *chilangos* (a semi-derogatory term used by Mexicans to describe people from Mexico City) in the mountains west of the city. I plied myself with so much tequila and music that I ended up doing judo rolls down the cobblestone streets of this picturesque mountain village. What a marvelous ambassador! I had stooped to the level of the Pacific Fleet on an overnight pass in Tijuana!

As most know, tequila occupies a special spot in the soul of every Mexican. After a few trips, I had decided that if I must drink tequila, it would be a good one, such as Herradura. We found ourselves having a "Harry" at Hacienda Los Morales one night while waiting for the perpetually late Arturo. Los Morales is a fine restaurant, the end result of the conversion of a wonderful old home. It sits on about four acres carved out of Polanco, Mexico City's answer to New York's Upper East Side. Hacienda Los Morales is a throwback to colonial days with expansive gardens and a wonderful sprawling hacienda. Arturo arrived, yes, late as usual (we Americans were stupidly forever on time), looked at our glasses and asked what we were drinking. We confirmed it was Herradura which Arturo then described as "dog piss" and called for the headwaiter. It hadn't tasted that bad to me, but I knew Arturo well enough that he was about to unveil a special surprise. The surprise arrived with an ancient retainer straining under the weight of a 50-liter keg, which he religiously placed at the end of our table. From the spigot, he poured glasses of 70 year-old tequila. It was wonderful, tasted like fine cognac and quite unjustifiably, has made me question the source of Herradura ever since.

There can be no family more generous than the Sanchezes. When in Mexico you could not pay for anything in their presence, and the frequency with which they presented gifts was almost embarrassing. One time, six of us were their guests for lunch in Taxco, an old silver mining town two hours south of Mexico City. It is a charming little historical town, clinging to the mountainside and complete with narrow covered alleys (often strips of canvas two or three floors up to cut the heat), an especially opulent church, a sunny central plaza and a plethora of shops selling silver. We looked at these endless displays of silver artifacts in our wanderings, but all of us had individually made the decision that an acquisition was not in our budget at that time. As we returned to the plaza, where our car had been sequestered with a guard during our absence, Dionisio presented exquisite silver bracelets to each of the three wives. He said, 'I didn't want you to leave such a memorable spot without a remembrance of it!"

Most Americans know Tex-Mex food, which is simple, tasty and fattening. Yet the Mexicans have some fairly unique and unusual food, the most notable of which is menudo, a tripe soup that to my way of thinking has absolutely no redeeming value. But then, stomach lining has never been my thing. However, someone a long time ago had to be either very hungry or exceptionally bold, for there are some pretty daring things that the Mexicans put on their plates that are a far cry from bean burritos. To my amazement, some were surprisingly good. Escamoles, sometimes referred to as Mexican caviar, are ant eggs, and as prepared by a knowledgeable chef, are better than good. Impoverished Indians in Guerrerro state, desperate for work, are coerced into putting their honey-coated arms into anthills to collect the ants (bulbous from their external eggs), which are then scraped from their arms. Apparently, these poor souls have been stung so severely that they can't work again for a week. This is a very tough way to make a peso.

The preparation of the Escamoles is key. The eggs (about the size of rice kernels) are simmered in garlic and butter, and then spooned onto a small tortilla along with dollops of guacamole and salsa. Perhaps the seasonings are better than the ant eggs, but I think not. The proof of this pudding is that a sister dish called *husanos* are large ringworms and prepared in the same way. They are no bueno!

Dionisio is very proud of Mexico, its culture and its people. I felt that he, in choosing foreign partners, wanted to assure himself that we shared his passion for Mexico. He wanted us to see his country in its best light, for so many Americans' image of Mexico is the more offensive or seamy side of the country. While in Mexico City just before Christmas, Dionisio announced that we would be going to a small town an hour north of the city to attend a pastorella. The little town of Topotzotlá is the site of a noted convent with palatial grounds and a substantial church fronting a large square, which, as in all small Mexican towns, is its focal point. A pastorella is a re-creation of Joseph and Mary's quest for lodging in Bethlehem on a long-ago Christmas Eve. Noted professional actors clamor for the opportunity to participate and play the roles of Jose and Maria in front of anticipatory crowds in the convent's main courtyard.

Perhaps three hundred of us awaiting the start of the play were seated at long tables in the patio while being plied with refreshments. After setting the tone, the cast leaves the convent through its huge wooden gates followed by much of the crowd. Recreating the couple's quest for lodging in Bethlehem, they go from door to door at the private houses facing the plaza. They, like Jose and Maria, are denied access by all. Ultimately, they return to the convent, followed by the crowd who is again seated to see the culmination of the Nativity scene. At the end of the play, servers bring huge platefuls of tamales and enchiladas to the tables and the feast begins. Pretty good tamales and enchiladas as a matter of fact. The Pastorella was a nice blend. It was a deeply moving experience combined with the joyful experience of a fiesta at the most important time of the year in Mexico. Again Dionisio was brilliant. Without doubt, he had shown off his country at its best.

THE WEDDING

Weddings are huge in Mexico. While in young Dionisio's office one day, I admired a picture of Dionisio and Olga at their wedding reception. They were surrounded by more roses than you could find in Pasadena on New Year's Day. I asked him about their wedding and he admitted, "Ours was fantastico, but wait until Arturo gets married".

Well, Arturo, the flamboyant son with the psychedelic corbatas, did get married, and to Mariana, a most gorgeous and cosmopolitan bride. There was never a doubt that the wedding would be a true happening, and receiving one of the 1100 invitations was thought to be a social coup.

The service was held in the spacious village church of Tlalpan, a pleasant little town that has been encircled by Mexico City's endless march towards becoming the world's second largest metropolis. The church filled one side of the square at Tlalpan, while shops and residences accounted for the balance of the frontage on this colorful and verdant little plaza. The Cardinal of Mexico was to officiate at the ceremonies, and as the good cardinal had been scarce in these quarters, a cadre of local onlookers had congregated for the occasion. It was a wonderful anomaly to see this church, filled with well-heeled and well-dressed invitees, play host to numerous street urchins sidling up the outside aisles to sprawl on the marble steps at the base of the altar for a front row view of the festivities. The vantage point they gained was well worth it.

For this evening wedding, the church was laden with white roses in stark contrast to the cardinal's crimson garment. Marianna wore a bejeweled dress with a seemingly endless train, and the groom, Arturo, never looked better. To the right of the altar were more than 20 members of the Mexico City Philharmonic in evening dress playing Bach and Vivaldi during the mass. Catholic masses are notoriously painfully long, but if this service was lengthy, it was so resplendent with its multitude of sights and sounds that the time passed as if a mere whisper. As Arturo and Mariana walked down the center aisle to leave the church, twenty mariachis resplendent in white ranchero suits lined the aisle and serenaded the couple on their walk to the front steps of the church leading down to the plaza. At that point, skyrockets pierced the night and their names; Arturo and Mariana were emblazoned on banks of scaffolding facing them as they left the church. The entire ceremony was an excellent proof statement that the Mexicans do know how to do things well.

If you have 1100 guests for a reception, you just don't hit up a friend to use his large backyard for the reception. They understand this in Mexico City, which has a number of halls constructed just for throwing large and lavish parties. The hall chosen by the Sanchez's would have put the old Palladium to shame. It came complete with tiered seating, lavish furnishings and a huge dance floor with an elevated bandstand. The hall also had developed the competency to serve a vast amount of excellent meals.

Arturo had warned the "gringo" contingent that we were not expected to leave the reception before seven in the morning, and American pride, being what it was, we were prepared to gut it out. We had no time to get bored or sleepy, no downtime whatsoever. With three constantly revolving dance bands, all night entertainment, a sit-down dinner at midnight and a buffet breakfast at 5:30 in the morning, our interest never flagged. Tequila flowed like spring water and the best Burgundies and Clarets were poured all night by each table's own private waiter. And just imagine; they served a very good Beef Wellington to 1100 sit-down diners. We were there until the bitter end at 8:30 in the morning and every one of the gringos agreed, as a fun party, it was at least an 8.0 on the Richter scale.

THE GENERAL

I met General William Fox through his nephew George, an old friend of mine. The General was a most unusual character. This small, wiry and high-energy man had more projects going than the United Nations. He had a similar personal appearance to the submarine advocate, Admiral Hyman Rickover, but from what I've read, the Admiral lacked much of the personality possessed in bucket loads, by General Fox. Before moving to San Miguel de Allende (pronounced San Mee gell day Aye YEHN' day) the wonderful hill town in central Mexico, General Fox had been County Engineer for the County of Los Angeles and from that base, seemed to know anyone worth knowing in the state of California. Even more interesting was his role as Marine Commandant of Henderson Field, the American outpost on Guadalcanal and scene of some of the bloodiest fighting in the Pacific during World War II. He would stay up nights and tell us stories of trying to prevent the "Japs" from sneaking their ships up "the slot" to supply their troops and of hand-to-hand combat in the jungle where he once was knocked over a 40-foot cliff by a bomb. He was especially complimentary of the Marine aviators under his command such as fellow pilots Pappy Boyington and Joe Foss, whose daring, courage and prowess made them aces in this very ugly theatre of war and household names back home where they were crying out for heroes.

A widower, General Fox retired from the county at age 60, sold all his possessions and headed for Mexico. With its clean air, 6,000-foot elevation and dramatic setting, San Miguel may be the most delightful small city in North America. Maybe Quebec or Santa Fe is in its league but their notoriety has brought them the de rigueur hordes of tourists. Sure, San Miguel has 2,500 gringos (many of them artists) among its 60,000 people, but you will have to look long and hard to find tour busses, T-shirt shops or horse drawn carriages. There is, however, an abundance of good restaurants and drinking spots, shops, bookstores and even language schools. Quite refreshing!

San Miguel de Allende sits on the flank of a mountain crisscrossed by

PETER MARR

high-guttered cobblestoned streets, which, in some cases, are so steep that rushing white water is created within them as it races down its flanks during their tumultuous summer rainstorms. Granted the town's outskirts are scruffy (the outskirts of all Mexican towns are scruffy) but as you enter, the whole aura changes; the buildings, though mostly single storied, almost overhang the narrow streets with their tightest of sidewalks. However, any feeling of confinement is redeemed by the open doorways, which usually give a hint of the shop, restaurant or home lying within. San Miguel is a town of parks, churches, markets and buildings colored in every shade of pastel known to man. *El Jardín* with its sculpted ficus trees facing the central square's colonnaded structures is also the stage for the engaging parish church, La Parroquia, whose wonderful carillon bells announce its presence every quarter hour. Outdoor cafes dominate the plaza, and one is entertained by wafts of conversations in many of the western languages as well as an occasional eastern tongue.

The Casa Sierra Nevada is a wonderful little inn perhaps three blocks from the Parroquia but well within the range of its bells. Several years ago, we spent two weeks there while attending the Allende Institute. The inn consists of three or four non-contiguous buildings anchored by the best restaurant in the state of Guanajuato. The chef is Swiss and the cuisine international, but its exceptional setting defines its charm. On warm nights you dine outside in a patio laced with jacaranda, bougainvillea and ivied walls, and the air is a mix of floral accents, herbs from the kitchen and just a touch of diesel from the street to assure you don't nod off. On inclement evenings, dinner is switched to a paneled dining room resplendent with paintings of the famous or near famous of Mexico, where, with the same food, same waiters and same casual dress, you experience a more formal tone. Either option was magical.

This is the town that General Fox, speaking no Spanish and knowing precious little about the Mexican culture, decided to call home. He was ready to assimilate. One newspaper observed, "He is an irascible old coot, stingy with his smiles, but he has a heart as big as a balloon and whether he likes it or not, he is a GENERAL!"

The General acquired a fine piece of property of three acres behind the Allende Institute and built a spacious home surrounded by the high wall that is customary in the area. In addition to expansive gardens, he built horse stables, corrals and a charo ring. He then began collecting horseflesh.

He was also busy elsewhere. The General amazed both the Latin and Anglo communities by deeply involving himself in the study of Spanish. It was almost an obsession, as this 60 year-old man mastered the language in an extremely short time. But this commitment was just another manifestation of a personality that demanded perfection, and he went a long way towards accounting for his position of prominence within both the Hispanic and Anglo sectors of the community

One evening over drinks, we were discussing the Spanish language. He said, "Wait one minute, I want to show you something". He bolted to his office, filled with memorabilia from the Pacific and returned with a small, dog-eared notebook. He thumbed through the pad until he came to a series of hand written notes. He said, "Look here, I have tried to note all the exceptions for the prepositions *por* and *para*. *Por* and *para* both mean **for** and I am told, are often misused even by native Spanish speakers. General Fox had listed over 80 exceptions of when one was used in lieu of the other. Talk about attention to detail. It is small wonder that the General became an unofficial (and unpaid) deputy to the *alcalde* of San Miguel and served as the spokesman for the foreign community.

His dedication showed on his rancho as well. He was learning charro. I would have loved to have seen that. Charro is Mexican rodeo and differs from ours. American cowboys spin the rope directly above their heads while in charro, the rope follows a huge circumference as the noose dives under the horse's nose and loops around the back of its tail. The America West's event of bulldogging differs from charro as well. In charro, the rider grasps the steer's tail, wraps it around his foot and then flips the animal. Tends to leave one with a serious limp if not executed perfectly.

The General was not intimidated and outfitted himself in garb that was a cross between a mariachi violinist and Emiliano Zapata. He became the only non-Mexican to ride with the Charros, a truly elite group of horsemen. He was never short for action, as his ring became the most attractive site for an impromptu chareada in the state of Guanajuato.

Better than ten years after first meeting the General, my wife Shirl and I shared a disheartening afternoon with him. We were traveling through San Miguel and paid an unannounced call on him. The movers were there and in the last stages of packing up the home that was now virtually empty. The General was justifiably a little melancholy but always the enthusiastic host. He had reached his mid-eighties and the lack of good medical facilities in San Miguel was forcing him to return to California to gain the care offered by the Veterans Administration Hospital not available in Mexico. He was resigned to it but not happy. General Fox had enjoyed 25 years in San Miguel, but in this minor way, paradise had let him down.

General Fox lived well into his nineties and touched all those that came into contact with him. Had he been born 400 years earlier he would have been a Sir Francis Drake as he was truly a leader of men, an explorer, a risk taker and a real live hero.

The Common Folk

The Mexico I have offered you to this point has been through the exploits and life of its privileged, its talented or both. It may be easy to love a place when much of your exposure and experience is through the eyes and deeds of the elite, but the qualities of the Mexican people are really exemplified by their poor. Separating yourself from your family by illegally crossing a dangerous border for work is heroic and so socially unnecessary. The Mexican poor have to take great personal risk to gain entry to a country that desperately needs their hard work and strong backs. Perhaps new leadership in both countries, who seem to want to cure the problem, will face it politically.

Where does this term "lazy Mexican" originate anyway? Not from any Mexican I have seen working in the states. Even with the Mexican peoples' troubles with crime and gang warfare here, they maintain an admirably close family unit and a terribly hard work ethic.

RAMONA

For over 30 years I have encountered many impoverished Mexicans in Baja California during countless off-road treks to that wonderful part of the world. Ramona was an entrepreneur who lived near Laguna Hansen at a remote settlement in the mountains of Baja, a hundred miles south of the border. She was short and dumpy, usually barefoot and her clothes and body received only occasional cleansings. Her hamlet was officially named El Asseradero, but if we knew that, we never called it that. It was always "the lumber camp" even though the commercial timber interests had long ago reaped their harvest of pines and moved on. It was approaching ghost town status, as there was nothing there but a dozen houses, a dirt soccer field where nobody ever played soccer and a tiny schoolhouse that never seemed to have any students.

That didn't appear to bother Ramona who always had a smile and possessed a wonderful disposition and a good heart. Her shanty was dirt floored and featured a potbelly stove that burned throughout the winter months, as this was high forest, not the desert usually associated with Baja California. Ramona sold candy bars, beer and soft drinks and most importantly, gasoline. Once a month, her husband drove the eighty or so miles on primitive road to Ensenada to restock. But it would be Ramona who would pour the gas from 40 gallon barrels into plastic milk cartons and in turn into our tanks, it was Ramona who would shoo the dog away from the fire on an icy day so you could warm hands so numb they had lost feeling and it was Ramona who was the cashier when it was time to get back up on the bikes and leave. She was tipped well. First of all we liked her, but as she maintained an outpost that catered to the off road community, all of us wanted to encourage her long-term success. I think we did.

PETER MARR

A Mountain Storm

A fierce thunderstorm turned a hot summer day into an electrical event in the mountains of northern Baja California. My biking partner, Dan Sweet, and I had been riding our motorcycles back towards the border from the southern deserts and were traversing a wide oak forested valley when it hit. Suddenly visibility was zero and the baked adobe road had taken on the characteristics of an ice rink. Thoroughly soaked we pulled off the road under a giant oak and cringed as the lighting crashed around us. A hundred yards below us was a rudimentary shack, and from its only door, a man beckoning to us. We dashed for the house dripping water and tracking mud through the modest but immaculate interior.

He had a wonderful wood burning fire going and some warm albondigas soup, and the combination of the two made us whole again. While none of us had much of a command of the other's language, we were able to communicate, and it became apparent his sole assets were the shack and two cows in the pasture facing us. He was worried about the well being of the cows in this storm. As soon as it abated, he made his apologies that he had to leave to check his cows but insisted we stay until we were dry, leaving us alone in his house. We never saw him again and when we left, we placed a twenty-dollar bill on his only table. I always had a strong feeling that we were wrong to have left the money. We had no sense that he ever thought that his kindness needed reciprocation, but we are Type-A Americans. We left the money. It made us feel better.

Once the dust of Mexico has settled on your shoulders, you can never shake it off.

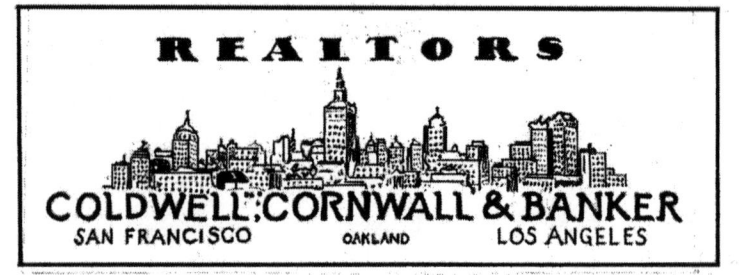

COLDWELL BANKER

REALTORS

COLDWELL, CORNWALL & BANKER
SAN FRANCISCO OAKLAND LOS ANGELES

"In the early sixties, Coldwell Banker was the most dominant and envied commercial real estate company in California"

REAL ESTATE 1A

COLDWELL BANKER AS IT WAS

Coldwell Banker was quite a company. In the early sixties, it was the most dominant and envied commercial real estate company in California. It enjoyed a camaraderie among its people rare then and even rarer now. Commercial real estate was coming into vogue, and Coldwell Banker was the place to work. The company certainly had no understanding of political correctness. Some would say, "What's changed?" There were no women on either the sales force or the management cadre, nor were any hired for another decade. Its ranks included very few racial minorities, but neither did its competition. Political correctness was still at least two decades away. Even personal computers were still twenty years away, and Xerox® machines and calculators were barely peeking over the horizon. The business was still conducted with slide rules, carbon paper and mimeograph machines.

Immediately after the San Francisco earthquake in 1906, Colbert Coldwell, later to be joined by Benjamin Banker, established a partnership: ultimately known as Coldwell Banker, which grew steadily through the first half of the century. Unlike a corporation, the twelve partners shared each other's liabilities, not to mention the liabilities of their 300+ employees. They trusted each other and a handshake was still a gentleman's bond. The "vibes" were good at Coldwell Banker which meant that it had a surplus of bright, aggressive young men who saw this company as either the way to financial success or, at the very least, the first step on the path to take them there. Most often they were entrepreneurial in spirit and opportunities on the commissioned sales force filled their needs for financial success. If not, they would leave for pursuits even more independent than Coldwell Banker could offer. In leaving, they became a part of a burgeoning alumni who would feed the company new potential business. Even to this day, most past employees proudly boast of their former affiliation with the firm. Those that stayed could also be extremely successful and would generate commission sales incomes that were the envy of their peers in other industries. Bill McAdam, a very popular chairman, used to boast that a dozen or more commissioned salespeople made more money than he did, and he was damn proud of that fact.

Getting a job at Coldwell Banker was a chore and a challenge. There were twelve partners: half in the Bay Area with the balance in Los Angeles. The founding of the company, right after the 1906 San Francisco earthquake, certainly was a propitious time to be in real estate, and growth was solid and sustained. By the end of the Great Depression, and somewhat to the chagrin of the San Francisco partners, the engine of the train had powered south to Los Angeles where the majority of the revenue was being created.

As part of the process of getting a job at Coldwell Banker, prospective employees were expected to interview with each of the Southern California partners as well as John Gilchrist and Bob Draine, soon to become senior managers of the firm. Most of us were young and fresh out of college or the military and were not considered qualified to move directly into a challenging sales position. We were interviewing for the opportunity to learn the business through the most menial tasks offered by the company: managing second tier commercial properties or financing homes. If the company liked you, in two to three years you were tapped for a sales job. The initial assignments were "grunt" jobs paying $300 a month but still highly contested among those seeking employment in commercial real estate.

Late in 1961, I was hired as a property manager and assigned to assist Bill Burnett, an old college friend, who, after a year's experience, was a virtual veteran. Our boss was Bill Sexton, a weak man, deathly frightened of the partners but emoting a self-important air with the "young bucks" that he was responsible for training. His trainees universally disliked him. One of Sexton's personal perks was a company car: a loaded Ford Fairlane that we all envied. To Sexton, the disadvantage of this perk was that he had been ordered to put it in a pool during the day so as to make it available to us minions to inspect our properties. Sexton loved to leave early on Friday evenings, but if the car was in use, he was hard pressed to do so. Every Friday, one of us sacrificed ourselves to the "Harass Sexton Movement" by signing the car out and not getting back to the office until 6:00 or 7:00 with an imaginary excuse to the seething Sexton that traffic, a recalcitrant tenant or a lease negotiation had delayed us. After a half a dozen such incidents, he blanked out Friday afternoon on the sign out sheet and took his car home early.

In the early 60's, Coldwell Banker was located on the top floor of the then prestigious Statler Office Building, an adjunct to the 15-story Statler Hotel in downtown Los Angeles. At that time, Los Angeles had imposed a 15-story height limit to all buildings except the City Hall for fear of earthquakes. Why the city hall received an exemption defies all logic. With new technology, admittedly some of which has yet to be field-tested, that limit has long been abandoned and buildings of up to 80 floors have been constructed in Los Angeles. Being attached to a hotel at the Statler was a godsend for us "new guys" as it housed a café and the very popular Seventh Street Bar. The business community had yet to learn that if you provided free coffee in the office you wouldn't have to deal with coffee breaks off-premises. You could keep your employees working rather than face their absence drinking coffee for a half an hour.

REAL ESTATE 1A

As novice real estate people, we loved to hobnob with the salesmen and learn about the trials, tribulations and potential triumphs that we would experience in the future. In retrospect, these coffee breaks were as integral to our training as was the 7th Street Bar after work.

"Vinny the Bartender" at the 7th Street Bar had a sparkle. The Coldwell Banker guys were among his best customers, and he never forgot any of our preferred drinks. "An Early Times on the rocks Bill, or your regular Dewars and soda, Pete?" He was uncanny. Sadly, too many of us drove home with way too much alcohol in our system. My brother Mike also worked for Coldwell Banker, and he and his buddy, Fritz Swinehart, found themselves downtown one night having had way too much to drink and facing a 40-mile drive home to Newport Beach. Mike owned the car so he drove. He manipulated the entire route in the right hand lane of the Santa Ana Freeway at 50 miles per hour. Nearly home, he caught up with a California Highway Patrol car also driving slowly in the right hand lane. Mike knew he had to make a value decision as to whether to pass him, and feeling it would be too obvious if he didn't, opted to pass. He did, only to be pulled over, spread-eagled on the trunk and then put through all the standard sobriety tests. From his vantage point in the passenger seat, his friend Fritz blearily peered out at this scene. The cop finally let Mike go saying, I could pull you in but your attitude and responses are much better than I expected. The patrolman asked Mike if he knew why he had been pulled over. When Mike said no, the cop replied, "Because the asshole sitting next to you flipped me off when you passed." I could editorialize on true friendship but I won't.

Silver-haired Art Wittenburg was one of the nicest and kindest men in the building. He was low-key (somewhat unusual for this bunch) and specialized in leasing downtown office buildings. He was a former FBI agent and obviously that occupation brings you into contact with some folks not qualified for canonization. Apparently this is how Art met Mushy Greenstein, a parking lot operator who leased parking lots all over the downtown area. At least weekly, Mushy would appear in the office along with his bodyguard, Jimmy Rist. Mushy was a small rat-faced man and

Jimmy a lumbering oafish type that reminded you of Lenny in Steinbeck's *Of Mice and Men*. Art knew all the owners downtown, so Mushy looked to him to find new locations. With California's love affair for cars, the demand for more parking lots never diminished. One of Mushy's lots was on the corner of 7th and Figueroa, right across the street from the Coldwell Banker office. When visiting Art, Mushy could keep track of the lot from the window, and one-day noticed a large truck blocking its entrance. Mushy turned to Jimmy Rist and said, "Jimmy, go get that truck the fuck out of the way; it's hurting business." Overhearing this preamble, several of us converged upon the closest window to see just how Jimmy was going to handle this. He approached the truck whose driver was sitting behind the wheel. Apparently the truck driver, who must have been a moron, questioned Jimmy's ancestry. Jimmy merely put one arm into the cab and pulled the hapless driver out through the window. He then held him about two feet off the ground (still with a single arm) propping him against the back of his offending truck where he proceeded to administer a very one-way lecture. When released, the truck driver peeled rubber in his haste to remove himself from the scene.

Our idol on the Coldwell Banker sales force was Fred Duckett. Fred was a tall, deliberate man who always looked like he was shrugging his shoulders as if to put on his jacket. He sold and leased shopping centers at the onset of their heyday, and no one knew them better than Fred. All of us knew that Fred had earned over $100,000 in commissions the prior year. Back in the early sixties this was huge, just huge, sort of like a racecar driver lapping the field or winning the Irish Sweepstakes on a £5 ticket.

Commissioned selling is one of the world's toughest ways to make a living. Every year you started with a goose egg next to your name on the earnings list and you survived, coped or prospered based on how clever, intuitive and hard working you were. It took guts, but as in Fred's case, the potential financial rewards could be very high. Fred, not the verbose type, tended to speak in short simple sentences. One day at his desk, he was leaning back in his chair with his feet on his desk listening on the phone to someone pepper him with questions. He had made lots of monosyllabic "yeps" or "nopes" as responses before sitting up straight in his chair and uttering, "No ma'am, no ma'am. Duckett, **D**-u-c-k-e-t-t." When Fred did leave Coldwell Banker he fit the mold established by those before him for continuing loyalty to the company. He developed a multitude of shopping centers that the company leased and/or sold for him. As successful as he had been as an employee, he generated far more revenues for Coldwell Banker as a client.

PROPERTY MANAGEMENT

I should explain what a property manager does. Since my experience in the early 60's, property management has become extremely sophisticated but as I've explained, for us it was just grunt work. We managed commercial buildings for others: usually absentee owners or investors who had acquired or inherited properties and for people who had either no interest or no capability to operate them. Coldwell Banker was hired to provide this service. While some of these properties were of good quality, many were in questionable locations with equally questionable tenants who had to be constantly prodded to pay their rent. One such property was the Adland and Geft holdings in the middle of the ghetto on Central Avenue in South Central Los Angeles. The word "holdings" may not properly describe this property. The building was maybe 50' by 100' and had two tenants. A beer bar, incongruously named Frenchy's, was located in the northern half of the building and when you walked inside you weren't exactly greeted with love and affection. We never went alone into Frenchy's and even after cajoling some of the ex-football players in the department to accompany us, we went with more than mild trepidation. The southern premises were occupied by what presumably was a record store but they only had a half a dozen ratty looking LP sleeves on display in the front window. Rent collection was not a problem here. The store was, in actuality, a very successful bookie joint! Predictably, the property did not survive the 1965 Watts Riots.

PETER MARR

The lowest property manager on the totem pole was assigned the daily "bank run." A year or so earlier, the bank run had replaced "sign truck duty" as the most menial corporate task. Things were more casual on the sign truck I am told, as you put on your Levis and drove all over Southern California placing For Sale or For Lease signs on the company's new listings. The truck was big enough to hold a surfboard and on occasion, Ron Wheatcroft or Bill Burnett had been known to bug out in the afternoon and "hang ten" at Huntington or Malibu.

All good things come to an end, however, so when I became the designated company rookie, I was assigned the mundane task of the daily bank run. All the company's rent checks, commission payments and property management fees had to be deposited. The first stop was to collect the deposit checks and slips from Bessie Tidey, the ever-popular accounting clerk. If I was lucky, I would get a grunt of recognition from the company's accountant, Bill Hall. Bill wore a green eyeshade that only partially covered the worst "rug" in the city. From the Statler, I walked east on 6th Street into the heart of the downtown. I stopped at the Bank of California, sometimes at the Bank of Los Angeles and always at the Bank of America. Two separate branches of Security Bank were used, one on Spring Street and one on Wilshire Blvd. I couldn't forget the United California Bank and for last, I always saved the Farmers and Merchants Bank way down on Main Street at the edge of Skid Row. (Interestingly, today only the Bank of America has survived, and it has been absorbed by a Carolina bank). I got to know the tellers, the cops on their beats, an occasional merchant and if I could spare a buck and a quarter I could get the city's best pastrami and Swiss on rye at the Yorkshire Grill on 6th Street. We got all of this plus the excuse to get away from the phones where tenants were calling complaining about leaking toilets and such things. Pretty damn good duty! I actually missed doing the bank run when Dick Clotfelter was hired off the Stanford campus and relieved me of duty.

Patsy Ferraro was a first generation Italian-American from Sicily. He was a handyman. When something needed fixing in one of our buildings we called Patsy. He would get the job done and while he didn't give away his services, he was reasonably priced and responsible. He also knew how to cultivate business. Every couple of months he would round-up all the young managers who didn't have a "pot to piss in" and take us to lunch at The Pantry, an ancient and funky "all you can eat" restaurant in the heart of the developing downtown area of Los Angeles. Every six months or so Patsy treated us to dinner at Martonis, a very good Italian restaurant purportedly owned by the mob in Hollywood. At Martonis Patsy was in his element, surrounded by his cadre of young Coldwell Banker go-getters, many of who later became hugely successful and who, for the price of a good dinner, would happily offer their fealty to an immigrant Italian. It was only perfect.

Patsy had a comfortable home in the Hollywood hills where he lived with his daughter, Maria, unfortunately an extremely homely woman. One day while driving down the Sunset Strip with Maria, he was lightly rear-ended by another car. Always mindful of personal injury law, he whispered to Maria. "Maria, bai-tah yur lippa, bai-tah yur lippa." Obediently she bit her lip, drew blood and Patsy settled with the insurance carrier for an easy $10,000.

THE PARTNERS

The partners were all equal, but Dick Mott was the most equal of all. He had the demeanor of a cigar store Indian and was tougher than construction nails but admired by all. He would go out and drink with the troops at night, but you were forever on his shit list if he beat you into the office at 7:30 the next morning. While he seldom avoided a good time, he bridged no crap either. At one of the company's annual outings to Dodger Stadium, Merilee LaMont, a very available secretary with an especially bounteous body, got a little inebriated and draped herself all over Mott. As spectacular as she may have been, Mott disapproved of the timing and the venue. Miss LaMont received her walking papers the following day! I knew that I had "arrived" at Coldwell Banker when Mott called me by my first name

PETER MARR

rather than "young man". That was my signal that he was now to be called Dick, and no longer "Mr. Mott," and I was probably permanently employed.

Louis Pfau was as patrician as Mott was plebeian. He was a slender man who dressed beautifully and had a pencil-thin mustache and an important distinctive demeanor. He was Pasadena society and generated a lot of business from the beautiful people like Buddy Rogers and Mary Pickford.

Bill McAdam, a colorful friendly former FBI agent, came from the San Fernando Valley, rolled his own cigarettes and was the ultimate man's man. Bill truly loved the troops, a love so obvious that it was immediately reciprocated. He ultimately became Chairman, undoubtedly the most popular chairman the company ever had.

Charles Detoy was balder than a cue ball and supposedly lost his hair from fright when stepping into an elevator shaft in a dark and empty building. Fortunately, the shaft was only a foot deep but the tonsorial damage had been done. Detoy was very civic minded and generated a great deal of business through his work on committees and governmental units. He knew not a whit about real estate but had enough people working for him who did, which was even more important. One of his best clients was Walter O'Malley, the owner of the Dodgers. I spent many hours with both of them looking for a west coast replacement for the Dodger spring training facility in Florida. It turned out to be a wild goose chase as, forty years later, the Dodgers still do their spring training in Vero Beach.

Dan Duggan was one of the younger partners and brought a law degree with him. He was a large man with an effervescent outgoing personality. Dan was an excellent judge of people and was often sought for counsel and for his insight and advice.

Denny Evans, the last of the Southern California partners, was a fullback on the Cal Wonder Team of the 20's. He was generally considered to be the only lightweight in the bunch as most of his business came from outside brokers he cultivated, almost a sin at Coldwell Banker. None of us grunts knew him well, as he was always with outside brokers.

The company incorporated in the mid-sixties and soon after went public, enabling those who survived the rigors of the job to enjoy comfortable retirements. There truly were some remarkable men who laid the groundwork for what ultimately became the world's largest real estate service company.

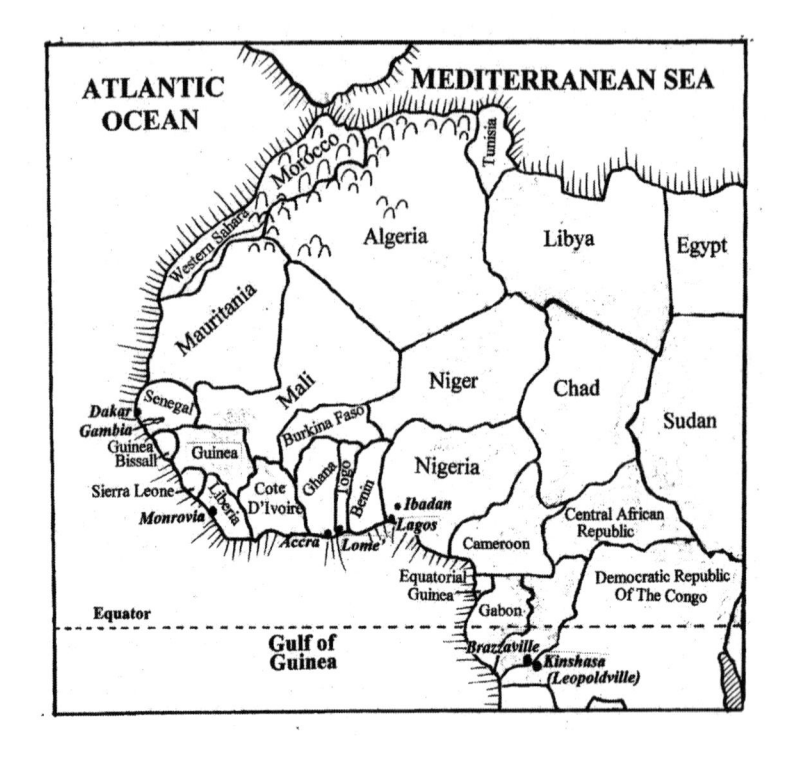

THE DARK CONTINENT

Sahara sunrises are intense. The sun almost explodes over the horizon bringing first its warmth but gradually and irrevocably transforming itself into the overpowering heat that is such a part of the King of Deserts"

THE DARK CONTINENT

INTO AFRICA

My first trip to Africa in 1960, gave me an ample flavor of this fascinating continent. I experienced its mystery, harshness, comedy and beauty as well as a touch of its devastating poverty.

I was a new Diplomatic Courier based in Frankfurt for the U.S. State Department. From Frankfurt, the Courier Service had 15 preplanned trips throughout Europe, Africa and the Middle East. Perhaps the least popular of the trips was the West African 102, which included the sub-Saharan countries of western Africa described by some as the world's armpit. Upon arriving, it was a continuous relay on third world airlines using antiquated equipment going to spots only the most seasoned of travelers would know. All this was done in stifling heat and using drip-dry shirts that might need laundering twice a day but were lucky to get it bi-weekly. But, it always was an adventure.

I left Frankfurt at eight in the evening on a BOAC propjet Britannia headed for Accra, Ghana. It was only my third courier trip and the first lengthy one as it lasted two weeks. It stopped at Rome and refueled at Kano, Nigeria, on the southern edge of the Sahara. Back in the fifties and

THE DARK CONTINENT

sixties, the flights always crossed the Sahara at night so the crew could use celestial navigation. Permanently placed vectors on the Sahara's surface didn't yet exist. I had 277 pounds of diplomatic pouches buried in the hold with, as always, security instructions that I be the last man on and the first man off the plane. In theory, this was to insure their safeguard. In Rome, at the modest old Ciampino Airport, we landed for a planeside pouch exchange before continuing southward over the Mediterranean and the Sahara.

Couriers are constantly crisscrossing destinations, so a pouch might be dropped with an embassy official who came to the airport or given to a marine guard or pouch clerk at the Embassy itself. Later they would be handed over to the appropriate courier going to their particular destination. So my inventory of pouches could be going most anywhere. Thus, a value decision had to be made by the courier to drop a pouch at the appropriate spot. This took no mental genius but did require a cursory knowledge of geography. In this instance, I had one pouch headed for Naples, which should logically have been dropped off at Rome and not at my ultimate destination, Accra. Shortly after leaving Rome, I discovered the Naples pouch, still resting in my working bag. Kind of dumb of me, what? Oh well, delivery would be only a week late, so I hoped Naples could wait. Maybe I would be lucky, and the only message in the pouch would contain a mundane new dress code policy for diplomatic receptions or something. I was never to know.

Incidentally, I learned that importance wasn't necessarily a criterion to get something included in the pouch. While couriers were not supposed to know what they were carrying, it was hard to miss a code machine or the like and an early arrival at the embassy's pouch room to pick up their inventory was often revealing. One Thanksgiving, I actually carried a frozen turkey into our embassy in Taiz, Yemen. Turkeys were hard to come by on the Arabian Peninsula.

I digress. Our landing just before daybreak at Kano on the Sahara's southern edge was almost surreal. As we landed, the first hint of an orange dawn slid over the horizon giving an inkling of the heat that was to follow. The plane needed to be emptied as the crew needed a break, the aircraft needed refueling and the passengers needed breakfast. My pouches were buried beneath the other luggage, thus being impractical to offload, so it was preordained that I spend the 90-minute layover under the plane on the tarmac. I did have entertainment, however. Saharan sunrises are intense. They begin in a coolness that you have difficulty associating with the Sahara. Then the sun explodes over the horizon bringing first its warmth but gradually and irrevocably transforming itself into the overpowering heat that is such a part of this king of deserts.

I experienced another wonderful Saharan sunrise almost 40 years later on holiday in Morocco. We rode bicycles to the end of the road that died at the Sahara's edge. There we transferred to camels and trekked into the desert. It was so quiet, so massive, so overpowering that we could have been days instead of a mere hour from the road. We spent the night in luxurious tents (perhaps another oxymoron) deep within the dunes. We had entertainment, great Moroccan tagine, (usually a dish of lamb with couscous, garlic, cinnamon, nuts, and fruits cooked in an earthenware crock often in your presence) passable wine and even odorless flush toilets. In the coolness just before dawn, a little man tapped on our tent pole and softly urged our attendance at the top of the tallest dune where coffee was being served. Again I experienced the exploding Saharan sun, but on this occasion, we were drinking imported Starbucks rather than chasing flies on the tarmac. Much more civilized! In addition, the camel trip was in February rather than August. You know the weather difference in Palm Springs from February to July—well, same-o same-o on the Sahara.

Back to the Britannia's layover in Kano. The town was immediately adjacent to the airport, and the muezzins were making their call to prayer from the minarets in that most penetrating and plaintive wail that they use. With the rising sun, the flies arrived and the spell was broken. Now these flies were bad hombres. Western Australia has some mean vicious little flies, but these Nigerian flies were more persistent than a telemarketer. I stood under the fuselage of the Britannia next to the hatch where my pouches were buried. The flies swarmed over me as if I were coated with honey until they had darkened my beige suit—and I mean darken; they covered it and me. After 30 seconds, I would sprint under the plane and have another 30-second respite before they again engulfed me. I bounced back and forth under the plane as if on a yoyo string, swiping, flailing, swatting, cussing and feeling very, very stupid. I only hoped I was far enough out on the tarmac that I wasn't noticed from the terminal. It was one frustrating 90 minutes, my welcome to Africa.

At nine that morning, we landed at the coastal city of Accra, (as in *Uh-krá,*) Ghana's capital. With my eighth of a ton of pouches in tow, I searched for a porter for assistance. It was the policy of the courier service to allow reimbursement of 25 cents per pouch for porterage. This was barely enough in western Europe and way too much in Africa—at least that was what I had been told by the senior couriers. My friend, Herb Moller, especially stressed that I was not to over tip and ruin it for the rest of them. They all declared the automatic 25 cents per pouch on their expense accounts wherever they were, but Herb told me that three to five cents per pouch was more than adequate in western Africa. Well, he really stuck it to the new guy. When I got to the embassy station wagon from the plane, I pulled out a shiny U.S. quarter for the three porters who had carried my 6 large pouches through customs and immigration. They immediately became agitated. I guess Herb had given me the wrong "scoop." Only my hasty search for a dollar bill brought smiles to their faces again. I learned, after a few trips, that 25 cents really wasn't enough in most of the places we went, so we usually bought the subsidized inexpensive cigarettes in the U.S. Army commissary in Frankfurt (Wow, but times have changed), and using them for tips made most porters very happy. In most third world countries, they turned around and sold them on the black market for a major profit.

From the airport, I was driven to the new modern embassy in Accra. With the Embassy closed for the weekend, I would sign the pouches over to the Marine guard. As many of the pouches would continue on with me or another courier to small embassies like Freetown and Monrovia, the bags were also small. These I had gathered together in my large working bag (it looked like a mailbag) for convenience. I handed over my invoice to the Marine, shook the pouches from my working bag and went through the paperwork of checking in more than twenty diplomatic pouches. I was short a pouch destined for Monrovia, Liberia. I felt the beginnings of a very queasy feeling in my stomach. No courier had **ever** lost a pouch (other than the four unfortunate couriers who had lost their lives and obviously their pouches in plane crashes) and here, I couldn't find the fucking Monrovia pouch. I shook the bag again with the same results. By this time, I was perspiring, and even Corporal Parks was getting a little edgy. Obviously, I thought, he didn't relish being the sharpshooter with the live ammo at my firing squad. The third time, I turned the working bag inside out and experienced a huge relief. There, along the bottom seam, was a wax sealed letter pouch stuck to the canvas! Accra was like Florida in August, and obviously the wax had melted en route and adhered to the canvas. I felt pretty damn good to have missed my own execution and happily bought Corporal Parks a bunch of very cold beers that night.

My carry-over goof of the Naples pouch was treated mildly. Louis J. White was the Regional Diplomatic Courier Officer back in Frankfurt. He was a former Postmaster in a Midwest hamlet and abhorred taking trips himself so stayed behind in Frankfurt tending his desk and his garden. Obviously, the traveling couriers did not universally admire him. His notation on my trip report was: "First time. Marr orally reprimanded and instructed in proper method". Whew!

With great celebration, Accra had just lost its colonial status but still evidenced some of the neatness and organization of the British. The city, a seaport, is located on Africa's underbelly south of the Sahara. The port would be called an embarcadero in Mexico as it wasn't much in size, and only small ships could enjoy a safe anchorage there. Bigger ships anchored a mile off shore and lighters, manned by as many as twenty oarsmen, brought the cargo to shore through the surf, a spectacle enjoyed by the locals who lolled around hoping for "spillage." East of the city was a tropical beach where my hotel had established a modest beach club staffed

THE DARK CONTINENT

with a beach boy to give you a towel and call for a car when you wanted to leave. That afternoon I visited this beach for some body surfing and assumed the $20 cash I was carrying would be safely hidden in the folds of my beach towel. Damn naïve if you ask me! But the beach was virtually empty and I was swimming only a hundred yards off shore, which justified my lapse. Back then, $20 was a year's wages in Africa which should have given me a small clue that the money would be gone upon my return. It was.

When I returned to the hotel, I reported the loss because I was American and we do things like that. Within two hours, the police appeared at my dinner table and politely asked that I join them in a room off the lobby. There, tied to a chair, was the beach boy. He appeared to have had the living shit beaten out of him. I was asked if this was the man who stole my money, a query I was unable or perhaps unwilling to answer. Justice (if there was such a thing there) was swift in Ghana. To this day I don't know what happened to the boy. It leaves a lingering distasteful feeling with me, for while he must have been the prime suspect, it was my sheer stupidity combined with the utter intransigence of the police, which had allowed the poor devil to come into harms way.

Lagos, the capital of Nigeria was the next stop. Nigeria has the largest population of any African country and either the Ibos or the Ebos (I never did know the difference) lay claim to being the best businessmen and often the worst rascals on the continent. I believe both parts of that equation. Even today, the Zulu and Xhosa, South Africa's principal tribes, claim that the Nigerians have taken over their drug trade and run the major crime syndicates in South Africa.

Lagos is not a memorable city. Several months later I had occasion to over-night there. I stayed at the Mainland Hotel, purportedly the best in the city. I assumed the predictable venue for an off-duty courier, a bar stool, and watched rats, which approached the size and ferocity of pit bulls, race behind the liquor bottles lining the back counter. Cut my thirst a bit.

PETER MARR

On my first trip, between flights, I ended up spending a very long afternoon in Lagos's small, empty and rustic airport. Today, a cyber cafe and curio shop would compete for your time and your cash. Then, the only merchant in sight was an Ibo, of an indeterminable age, selling exquisitely carved ebony heads. Looking for a diversion, I started bartering for a large carving which I had absolutely no way of carrying with me. That did not deter either of us. I offered $2 and was countered with $60. A half an hour later he was at $30 and I was at $15. It was time to play my trump card. I pulled off my watch, a vintage Timex (it had cost me $8.50), and offered it even across the board for the head. What a coup! He seemed impressed. He held it high and inspecting it as if with a jeweler's loupe. Finally he lowered the watch, packed up his carved heads and dismissed me with the statement, "no deal, no jewels"! I didn't want to carry the damn thing all the way through Africa anyway. I had been bested by the best.

The southern terminus of Route 102 was Leopoldville in the Belgian Congo. For a number of years after "independence", the Congo was known as Zaire. Zaire received some notoriety from Mohammed Ali as the site of his championship fight with George Forman, but today its name has reverted to the Democratic Republic of Congo. On my first visit, it had just gained its independence from Belgium, and Zaire was already well into its first civil war.

Maybe none of the European powers had been great overseers during their African ownerships, but, by and large, the self-government that followed colonialism has been unsuccessful as well. The French left a culture and the British a structure, but the Belgians left chaos when they turned this richest of countries back to the people. The people simply were ill prepared to operate this asset. I seem to remember that there were less than 20 college graduates in the country's entire native population!

Leopoldville, now known as Kinshasa, was situated on the southern banks of the massive Congo River and laid out in a pleasant European manner. It was bisected by an attractive boulevard with a wide grassy divider and

THE DARK CONTINENT

was fronted by businesses, offices and even outdoor cafes. You generally entered Zaire from the airport, but as rebel forces were surrounding the city, the airport was closed. Directly across the river was another Congo, this one run by the French and much smaller in size and influence than Leopoldville. But it had a city with an airport that was open, Brazzaville. We would arrive in Brazzaville late in the day, but with enough time to enjoy some fine French food and wine, before retiring to spend the night under mosquito nets. No wonder the couriers had barrages of inoculations. We regularly received shots for everything from cholera, yellow fever, and the plague—injections ad nauseum.

The following morning I picked up my pouches at the Brazzaville Embassy—lots of them—for, with the Congo at war, diplomats and their minions find a lot of things to report. I was then taken to the ferry landing to cross the Congo (seven miles at this spot) to Leopoldville on the southern shore.

The boat was jammed with Congolese on their way to a war zone. This always confused me. I thought that natives fled war zones. The boat looked like it had appeared along with Hepburn and Bogey in the "African Queen". You must have seen the pictures of the Tokyo subway where specially hired employees of the railroad are assigned to shove passengers aboard? This was the maritime equivalent. There was one other westerner aboard, a correspondent from the Irish Times arriving to cover this ugly little war. The crossing, which weaved through flotsam the size of small villages, went smoothly until we landed at the Leopoldville docks. A week old government, whose country was under siege, was operating Passport Control! While the natives poured ashore, the Irishman and I were denied entry by a sergeant who had probably been mining tin a week earlier. He explained (well, sort of explained) that we needed a visa to enter Zaire. We then determined that the only place visas were issued was in downtown Leopoldville. It was clear that this sergeant was a co-author of Catch-22. After half an hour arguing with most of the Congolese Army, I sent the embassy driver back for help. He returned with the Deputy Chief of Mission (DCM), the individual second in command to the

Ambassador. After another half hour, and a small donation, we were granted entry. Had I thought of "the small donation" earlier, we surely could have speeded up our entry but would have missed out on seeing democracy in action.

Back at the Embassy, I was informed that I would spend the night at the Memling Hotel, which was acting as the UN Headquarters. I was also warned by the DCM, that the capital, while outside the war zone, was volatile, and I should expeditiously remove myself from any congregation of people. Was it Noel Coward who said that only mad dogs and Englishmen go out in the mid-day sun? Well, I have been known to bark! At a civilized lunch hour, I found myself and maybe five other hardy souls on the main avenue checking out the environment and having a cold Stella Artois at a sidewalk café in the glaring sun. The street was empty except for one bicyclist and one Army truck. They met. The truck hit the cyclist at a fairly high rate of speed, threw the unfortunate devil onto its hood and most obviously dispatched him to a better world. Instead of waiting for the police, the Army private who had been driving the truck, saw what he had done and ran across the boulevard and headed directly for the café where I had been enjoying my well deserved Stella. From what had been an empty landscape, suddenly the buildings and streets had eyes, and people by the scores emerged to intercept the hapless driver. He went down on the sidewalk in front of the café, and was pummeled and kicked by this angry mob from hell. I later learned he had been mortally wounded by the throng, an event I did not witness, as I had heeded the DCM's advice and had removed myself with all dispatch from the site. I even stiffed the café for the better part of a Stella and the yet-to-be served lunch. I doubt they missed me in the melee.

The Memling Hotel was a classic. It was a well-landscaped three story concrete building right in the heart of town. It might have been a throwback to a Somerset Maugham novel or even the Olafson at Port au Prince in Haiti made famous by Graham Greene. The UN had sent diverse forces to the Congo to prevent a civil war, but Africa never rated the same response that a Kosovo or Kuwait justified later in the century. The hotel was jammed, and a bribe was necessary to get into the dining room. A polyglot of languages were being spoken and international military uniforms peppered the lobby. Obviously the Irish were in attendance, otherwise, why send a correspondent to Zaire. My Irish Times friend from the ferry ably provided endless expense account whiskies, more than a fair trade-off for getting him into the country on my shirttails. After the Irishman had left, the barman cheated me out of ten dollars—a lot of money to me then. The manager was sympathetic but said I was on my own. There was no way he could discipline his employees under the new order.

The rest of the trip worked its way back towards Europe. More layovers in Accra and Lagos and endless flights on hot, lethargic DC3s with stops at such garden spots as Conakry, The Gambia, Sierra Leone and Lomè. The last African stop was Dakar in Senegal, the closest point of Africa to the Americas. The French had run Senegal, and they had developed Dakar into the most attractive city in Western Africa. It was on an expansive bay in a very handsome setting. The Air France hotel was comfortable and efficient and was spotted on a marvelous stretch of beach. The following day I had plenty of time to enjoy some of the best, uncrowded body surfing I have ever experienced.

The opulent treatment on the Air France 707 jet to Paris that evening made its indelible statement that I had left Africa behind me. The plane was fast, efficient and luxurious; all things that Europe was and Africa wasn't. Departure was a dichotomy:

>Hard to leave,
>Easy to leave.

THE ENGLISH
GOD BLESS THEM

BEACHFIELD

"With my first glimpse of England, I knew I was destined to be a life-long Anglophile"

THE ENGLISH

GOD BLESS THEM

From my very first glimpse of England in 1953, I knew that I was destined to be a life-long Anglophile. "Mind you", as they say, I didn't set foot on one of the isle's more scenic spots. Tilbury Docks sits across the Thames from Gravesend, a most apt description of the area. Let's face it, East London ain't pretty and makes Detroit look like Disneyworld. But it looked great to me. Ten days on the rough North Atlantic aboard a Liberty ship converted for student traveling has a way of making anything that passes for terra firma look awfully good.

London is a series of cities within a city: Mayfair, Kensington, Chelsea and even Westminster were smaller towns that, over the centuries, were absorbed by the square mile City of London, the result being greater London as we know it today. From the docks, our double-decker bus crept westward towards central London traversing through mindless blocks of East End row houses, fish and chip emporiums and newsagents with handmade paper signs in the windows. This was postwar Britain. We were mesmerized by the still existent bomb craters with hosts of shrapnel scars, their partners in crime, all still in evidence. Gaps that were once buildings, fatalities of the German buzz bombs, were still commonplace eight years later. Even today it is easy to spot those real estate casualties of the war, as they have usually been replaced by non-descript 1950's architecture that fares poorly when compared to its more classic predecessors.

We entered the bustle of the City of London. It is London's most notable city within a city as well as being the location of the Stock Exchange, Liverpool Station and the Bank of England. The neighborhoods adjacent to the newspaper offices of Fleet Street were stacked with pubs. They abated a bit through Holborn, but by the time we passed through Soho, the theatre district, they were back with a vengeance. Now this was England I thought. Names like the "Rose and the Thorn", the "Bull and the Bush" and "Ye Old Cheshire Cheese" rang with antiquity and romance, strange bedfellows for a California boy. Finally we were in Central London and the benumbing grandeur of Big Ben, Parliament and the Westminster Abbey. I immediately knew that if I hadn't fulfilled all qualifications for membership as an honorary Brit, I certainly had absorbed enough empathy for this wonderful city to become one. I still feel that way.

LIVING IN LONDON

I was to come to learn about London first hand when Shirl and I leased a flat on Queensgate between 1997-99 while I was on a European business assignment. Our familiarity with the British taught us that even though we share a common language (some would say in spite of the fact we share a common language), Yanks and Brits do differ substantially. Early on, Peter, my then two-year old grandson, exemplified this. On a rare warm winter day, we took him on a walk to Hyde Park. Children were everywhere, kicking balls, flying kites, sailing model ships in the Round Pond. A soccer ball suddenly appeared at Peter's feet, and he did what any American kid would do; he threw it back to a group of British children. They were in awe as he had **thrown** the ball! They played together for twenty minutes, and the British children never threw the ball and Peter never kicked it.

PETER MARR

It is hardly a secret that London is a very cosmopolitan city in which to live. Expensive, yes, but cosmopolitan. We experienced this first hand when letting our flat near the park. We never did learn how we should geographically classify our Queensgate location, so usually described it as "just three doors off Hyde Park". Our postal zone put us in South Kensington, our local government was in Westminster, the nearest High Street was Kensington and the maps said Knightsbridge. Our neighbor, James Blamey, said he liked to take his pick dependent upon the moment.

Most Americans calculate that if something costs a dollar in the states, it costs a pound in London. For the past several years, it has cost in the vicinity of $1.50 U.S. to buy a pound. Thus, if it costs three dollars in the states to buy a cappuccino, it costs three pounds in London. British Airways did a promotion every holiday season exhorting the British to fly to New York to do their Christmas shopping. Those who have succumbed to the "adverts" claim the savings on purchases in New York more than makes up for the costs to fly and stay there. Perhaps it's aimed at people with "comfortable" incomes like Sir Elton John or the Duke of Marlborough, but the number of comfortable people living in London is vast. Just stop in Harrods any day and watch the bushels of money disappear into the coffers of Mohamed Al Fayed, Harrods's slightly flawed and addled owner. You remember, he's the guy who wanted to be Lady Di's father-in-law and still claims the C.I.A. assassinated her!

There are some surprises when you move into a flat in the U.K. There are no electrical outlets in the loos; against the law. Most of the washer/dryers are front loaders and small, and after several hours determining how they work, you discover they will take several hours to anguish through a load. The "telly" doesn't come free either. The government charges an annual connection fee of £120 a year per television set. If you watch BBC1 or BBC2, it is undoubtedly justified, as the revenue raised from the fees is used specifically to underwrite these two commercial free stations of the government-owned British Broadcasting Company.

Having a car in London is discouraged and in retrospect, with some justification. First, virtually no flats come with garages and if they do, expect to pay upwards of £300 per month to house your car. The local governments do have an uncanny method of pleasing their resident car owners, generating tax revenue, fortifying private industry and finally providing the locals with some amusing entertainment. It works like this:

    a) The City of Westminster issues an annual parking permit for £75 that entitles you to preferential parking from 6AM to 8PM. However, to prove that you are worthy of this perk, the form requires that you have a testament to your character by an attorney, a clergyman, a Member of Parliament or your banker. I told the clerk at the Westminster City Hall that, as I was new to the country, such a testimony might prove difficult for me to obtain. Being typically and wonderfully English and anxious to break through red tape, she asked if I had a bank account. Fortunately my bank had a branch next door where the manager gladly attested to a lifelong knowledge of my outstanding character. My God, I'm glad they had never seen my behavior on a golf course!

    b) The City of Westminster gains a benefit as they receive revenue for the use of their streets from the generation of a huge number of parking fines. The British motorist never seems to tire of trying to "beat the system".

    c) The City retains a towing service to patrol the most congested parking areas and even though the towing company underwrites the constable aboard, the private sector collects a hefty towing fee and profit.

    d) The amusement comes when the tow trucks arrive. These are flat bed lorries with a rotating grappling hook mounted behind the cab. They edge up parallel to the offending parked car, attach chains around all four wheels, attach the lift to the chains and then hoist the car onto the bed of the lorry. As our street, Queensgate was around the corner from the busy Royal Albert Hall, and as the warning signs were not conspicuous, it was a lush playground for these modern day highwaymen. On a summer's evening we might have as many as three lorries working our block. We would sit on our balcony (often sipping a single malt) and compare the efficiencies of the lorry drivers, for, as the street was tree-lined, it was not uncommon to see cars ricocheting off the tree trunks resulting in the old malady, "bark on the bonnet". Often, we had to be the bearer of sad tidings, for when the owners would return to find neither car nor note, we would have to tell them where the towing yard was and that they would need to pay £175 to retrieve a car sometimes not worth much more than that.

Pubs, bars, bistros, cafes and restaurants

Drinking establishments in London run the gamut: anything from the rowdy working man's pubs in East London (or any other part of town for that matter) to martini bars in the west end. In between you could get a drink in neighborhood pubs, business pubs, hotels, restaurants, private clubs, gambling clubs and even department stores. London was an alcoholic's nirvana.

Everyone seemed to have his or her favored neighborhood pub. Shirl's and my favorite was Ennismore Gardens, and we seriously scouted the greater neighborhood before adopting "our pub". Its clientele was a mix of college students from the abutting Imperial College, local residents, members of the staffs of the embassies that proliferated this area and an occasional drop-in. Half the fun was getting there, as the 10-15 minute walk from our flat took us by the Royal Albert Hall, the Royal Geographic Society, several embassies, through the dormitories and quad of the

THE ENGLISH

college and finally through a series of mews. (Mews, very common in London, were the former stables for the homes of the affluent, which often have been gentrified to become very comfortable residences). Our direction beacon to Ennismore Gardens was the always-lit Harrods, which loomed over the rooftops several blocks away.

The brewers own most English pubs as a means of getting their product directly to the market. They have full-time managers, sometimes housed on the premises, who in most cases take a real pride of ownership. They offer all types of spirits but their mainstays are beers and ales. The most common are lager (the lightest in texture and served chilled), bitters (true ale that is generally served at room temperature) and stout, a heavy strong dark beer or ale. They all can be bought by the glass, the pint or the pitcher. The Ennismore Gardens pub had been destroyed by bombs during the blitz and proudly portrayed pictures of its predecessor on its walls. Its ivy-covered exterior blended with an interior of old prints, soft lighting, a dartboard, the ever-present telly and a food station for basic sandwiches and light meals. After a number of visits we were accepted as regulars and rewarded them with our loyalty. I would kill for an Ennismore Gardens back home!

Now Duke's is quite a different kind of establishment. Dukes has perfected the art form of martini making to such a level that it would bring a smirk to the face of James Bond were he to watch one built there. The bar is part of the small venerable Duke's Hotel located in a maze of alleys and narrow lanes in St. James, a wonderful mixed business and residential neighborhood between Piccadilly and the Palace. Actually, many of London's best clubs are located within its boundaries as well as St. James Palace, the former home to the Royal Court and the home of the late Queen Mum.

Duke's is memorable because of Gilberto the bartender. Gilberto is Italian born but very British in demeanor. He appears at your table with his own small stand, a cutting board, an atomizer of vermouth, several lemons, an assortment of olives and the specific bottle of vodka or gin you have

85

requested. God forbid one should order a martini on the rocks for while he would politely construct one for the offender, he would consider it offensive and deign the customer a fool for adding ice to such a magnificent concoction. The preparation is a spectacle. Gilberto, with the formal bearing of the English combined with the flamboyance of his Italian heritage, has you mesmerized by the process. The chilled glass is given center stage. He sprays it with vermouth, pours the spirits directly from their chilled bottle (no shaking or stirring by Gilberto) then slices a long curlicue of lemon peel, which he uses to spritz the glass before gently lowering it into the finished product. It is not unusual to hear applause upon his completion. As more of us spread the secret of Gilberto's prowess, it led to growing popularity, and the hotel relocated a sitting room in order to enlarge the bar. Gilberto dictated the need for more tables. He says, "The only civilized way to drink a martini is while seated." Gilberto is to a martini as Shakespeare is to verse.

The old story about the difference between heaven and hell certainly exposes one of Britain's former great weaknesses: cooking. It is said that heaven consists of British police, French food, German engineering and Italian lovers, all run by the Swiss. Hell, on the other hand, consists of British food, French engineering, German police and Swiss lovers all run by the Italians!

Granted, you can still get some real "English" meals in London with black pudding, mushy peas, well done roast beef and sour rhubarb pie, but the state of London cooking (with a lot of eclectic help from Asia and the continent) has become outstanding. London restaurants now compete for their stars in the Michelin Guide, and entrepreneur Terrance Conran has even exported his bill of fare and operational genius to New York and Paris. In London, you can find everything from Indian to Italian; from casual to upper crust.

Possibly the most snobbish entrepreneurial chef in London is Marco Pierre White. Anyone who insists on using three names, each in a different language, has to be more than a little vain. He does, however, have a number of highly rated restaurants in London including Mirabelle and Canteen. Richard Lay and Anthony Turnbull, two of the most quintessential Englishmen I have ever known, were at the Canteen one night for a business meeting with clients. They had requested a window seat on the river. They were ushered to an inside table and mildly complained that this was not what they had reserved. The headwaiter said he would try to remedy the situation. He did. Several minutes later, he returned and asked them to leave. He stated that Marco Pierre White felt that the Canteen had no room for people who questioned the operation, and he no longer wanted them in his restaurant!

Perhaps we were lucky for on the only occasion we ate at the Canteen, we were unaware of either this incident or of the existence of Marco Pierre White (interestingly, it is never Mr. White or Marco, always Marco Pierre White) so we made dinner reservations to celebrate my wife Shirl's birthday. Our good British friends, the Blameys, together with old friends from California, Phil and Evie Cutting, accompanied us. Phil is an audacious extrovert with definite bombastic qualities, and all who know Evie feel she is a very short step shy of canonization just for persevering with Phil. Some twenty years earlier in Paris we had tried to get reservations at a popular local eatery, Le Soufflé. The concierge at our modest hotel had been unable to get a commitment until Phil asked to talk to the headwaiter. He explained on the phone that he was General Cutting and would require a table at 8 PM. He got the table and when Phil showed up in "civvies" that evening, he feigned a very impressive military bearing for a ROTC product. "The General" couldn't have been any prouder of himself.

By the end of our dinner at the Canteen, having substantially depleted its wine cellar, it was time for dessert. At this point, Phil began clinking his glass (perhaps it was more of a chime with such expensive crystal) to get his fellow diners' attention. The crowd hushed, the waiters froze and the headwaiter frowned as Phil's conduct was highly extraordinary. Fortunately Marco Pierre White was in the kitchen painting essence of truffles and pâté onto saltine crackers (or some such thing) and was unaware of this fuss in his establishment. Phil, in his stentorian voice, advised the diners that it was the birthday of the beautiful lady on his right (Shirl by this time had shrunken into a small ball at the back of our banquette) gave a short biography of the birthday girl, admitted that he was from the states (which seemed not to surprise anyone present) and asked that all join him in singing Happy Birthday to this most beautiful lady. He then added his coup de gras, "And God bless England."

Well, stuffy restaurant or not, that last comment energized what turned out to be a very affable crowd who broke out in a birthday serenade to Shirl. On our way out, diners stopped us to talk and even the waiters (you can be sure out of sight of Pierre Marco White) went out of their way to express their pleasure.

THE LONDON TUBE
AND OTHER LOCAL TRANSPORTATION

Shortly after I first met Shirl, she was wearing a T-shirt she had bought in London, which pictured a map of the London Underground on its front. Now Shirl is especially well endowed which meant that as the cloth stretched, so did the map. I had never realized it was so far from Pimlico to Victoria Station!

The Underground is a fascinating but aging (parts are 140 years old) subway system that is the backbone of London. Where else can you behold such a warning as "Mind the Gap" or be entertained at the base of escalators by musical groups of up to 5 or 6 minstrels whose sole source of income is a strategically placed hat or Styrofoam cup? The Underground served as the world's largest air-raid shelter during the Second World War. It is affectionately known to all as "the tube", and not unlike California's recent struggle with a neglected electrical grid, the system is overtaxed, somewhat unkempt and in need of a lot of capital to make it crisp again. During rush hours, as unpredictable as it may be, the Underground is usually faster and certainly less expensive than surface traffic. You never know if you will arrive at your destination refreshed or as a basket case needing immediate libation. Some trains are so jammed that you are forced to wait for the next one, but letting too many pass may require you to take up permanent residence in the Oxford Circus station.

The London taxi system is the best in the world. As the cabs are clean, the pay good and most of their fares derived from a polite and reasonably well-behaved society, driving cabs has become a coveted job. In order to pass the rigorous exam to be a licensed driver, taxi trainees take up to three years memorizing every street, hotel, station, mews, park and business establishment within a seven-mile circle of Charing Cross Station. In all weather (and no one has ever claimed that English weather is good), you constantly see motorbikes with big red L's (for Learner) on their tail and a map perched on their petrol tank cruising back streets of London and making grease pencil notes on the Plexiglas cover of their map. These are cab drivers in training. Once accepted, they are uncanny in their ability to find most any location. One elderly cabbie actually refused to accept a fare from me when he couldn't remember the location of Mayfair's two block long Stratton Street!

The London double-decker bus is an intriguing way to get around town. From the upper deck you have a unique view of the city. Cruising by Hyde Park you get a dirigible's view of fountains, monuments and horse trails, and are privy to a fine overview of the strategy being used on the numerous soccer fields within its confines. You flirt with smugness from your lofty perch on the second deck as you peer down on the masses of humanity congregating on Oxford Street or Piccadilly Circus. You might witness a "mum" pushing her newborn in a pram bigger than a Morris Minor or even bus by the Ritz and observe bellmen loading the hotel's Bentley with palettes of Fendi luggage to transport a French countess to Waterloo to catch the speedy Eurostar through the "Chunnel" back to Paris.

Being a conductor on the Number 9 bus doesn't pay as well as being a taxi driver. No tips, standing all the time and the need to squeeze his way through narrow aisles to collect fares while trying to dig change for £20 out of his pocket inside a sardine tin does not get many votes for "job of the year"! Some conductors are a little bit surly, but the great majority take pride in their work and are actually protective of their brood. One time in Knightsbridge, I saw a Pakistani conductor face down two large thugs on his bus, and kick them off accompanied by his shouts declaring them as known pickpockets (I think he called them "dips"). His cries resounded down the street as the dips slunk in quick retreat down a cramped alley. The conductor got a well deserved round of applause from his passengers.

The Naval Officer

Earlier I mentioned James Blamey, our Queensgate neighbor. James (note they have few Jims in England but lots of James) was a Sandhurst graduate who was assigned to her Majesty's Royal Navy where he spent the better part of ten years. While in advanced training at Sandhurst, he and his fellow officers were invited to a well-chaperoned dance at a nearby exclusive girl's finishing school. There he met Daniella, a stunning blond from the north of Italy and as the British like to say, was smitten. Daniella's initial reaction was not flattering she said, but after James persisted, she agreed to see him at the dance the following week but only if he produced on his boast to learn 100 words of Italian before then. She felt that she had seen the last of him. Back at the base, the only English-Italian dictionary available to James was from the motor pool, but it was filled only with Italian automotive words. The following week he learned an Italian vocabulary of 100 words (basically limited to the definitions for carburetor, transmission, differential and such), and upon his return to Miss Pratt's (it must have been a name like that), James's linguistic skills obviously greatly impressed Daniella, now Mrs. Blamey.

Prior to its decommission James served a tour as navigator on the Queen's yacht, the 450 foot *Britannia*. While the royal family was not often in attendance, the crew serviced a steady flow of family members, royalty and VIPs. Elizabeth's mother, the Queen Mum, enjoyed the yacht almost as much as she enjoyed her martinis. She didn't like drinking alone, so the young officers were rotated to have pre-dinner martinis with the

Queen Mum. She always had two and sometimes three martinis "up" and not an officer aboard could match her drink for drink.

The *Britannia* had a small bridge, with a large Captain's swivel chair featured in its center. Orders were that the chair was to be used only by the captain or the Queen should she find her way to the bridge. However, on drawn-out graveyard shifts, the comfortable chair was a temptation and the junior officers of the deck often used it when things were especially quiet. One night as James was finishing the midnight to two shift, his replacement appeared at the back of the darkened bridge, saw the chair occupied and assuming that James was again bending the rules, walked up behind and started tweaking his ears intoning in a sing-song falsetto, "Who's that naughty, naughty boy, sitting in the captain's chair?" It's occupant, not being James, turned around, peered at the young lieutenant and said, "It is I, Prince Philip!" The Queen's consort had been unable to sleep and, being an ex-Naval officer himself, had headed for the comfort of the bridge. Prince Philip took it completely in stride but the young lieutenant was in a state of shock for several days.

THE RENAISSANCE MAN

Anthony and Petronel Turnbull are very English. To be absolutely correct, and Anthony is correct, the pronunciation is *An' tony* (leaving out the aitch). Petti, Petronel's shortened nickname, is used only with family and the closest of friends. But make no mistake; stuffiness is not a part of this couple's English psyche.

My first encounter with Anthony and Petronel was in the company of several American associates celebrating the finalization of a partnership between our respective companies and countries. We were dinner guests at the Turnbull's former home in Cobham, a village in Surrey just southwest of London. This home was a former stagecoach stop and was well over 400 years old. Prior to our planned dinner with the Turnbulls, we were guests at Twickenham, England's most hallowed rugby grounds in London's western suburbs. We attended the Twickenham Sevens, which was more of a carnival than an athletic contest. The English like to say that soccer (or football as they prefer to call it) is a game for gentlemen attended by hooligans, while rugby is a game for hooligans attended by gentlemen. There is some truth to it.

The shortened rugby games were played on a round-robin format using only seven players per side (thus the Twickenham Sevens). This generally led to a faster more exciting contest than found with the standard 11-man format. The tournament started in the late morning and went until early evening. Stamina was important for both participants and spectators. Between spring rainsqualls, the spectators would yoyo between their seats and the parking lot where the damndest tailgate party I have ever seen was taking place. By comparison, it made California's UCLA-USC tailgates look like afternoon teas. It featured outlandish outfits, lavishly catered feasts, social register types acting like buffoons and more drunks than Skid Row on Saturday night. We fit in quite well, and as a result, we were a little boisterous when we arrived in Cobham for the Turnbulls home-cooked English dinner. Our attorney, Greg Spinner, who was with us at Twickenham, had just discovered the word "pissed", a pub word that is a quasi-acceptable (although perhaps socially objectionable) term for being drunk in England. As a result, none of our hosts were immune to his braggadocio that he was "really pissed". He was, but so much for a great start with your new partners!

While Petronel was an excellent cook, English home-cooked dinners were usually uninspiring and included some kind of overdone boiled meat, overdone boiled vegetables with pudding for desert. Sanity again prevails after dinner when cognac and cigars make their appearance. During such a cigar fest, my good friend Tad Jones again evidenced his uncanny way of seizing center stage. While Anthony espoused Chaucer and read aloud from a 400-year-old book of menus (even as charming and erudite man as Anthony had his down times), Tad turned his attention to Emma, the very comely girl friend (and now wife) of the Turnbulls' son, Timmy. She was a wind surfing instructor and at last count, there are no ugly wind surfing instructors. Those of us accustomed to the man were admiring Tad's gift of gab at the dinner table. Suddenly however, Emma let loose a scream .... **TAD!** Conversation halted while all eyes turned to Emma who was starring at Tad with a look of chagrin on her face. Innocently, Tad was inspecting his fingernails well above the table. Emma's consternation had no doubt been as a result of her assumption that the movement in her lap had been other than the family cat, Mogadishu, who had made an unannounced landing there from beneath the table! Ah, sweet vindication.

Both Anthony and Petronel have had great success in life. Petronel is a magistrate, the English counterpart of the American justice of the peace, and now sits in weekly judgment at the courts in Newport on the Isle of Wight. Anthony, a retired property executive, is retired in name only. He has more irons in the fire than he ever did as Chief Operating Officer of Debenham, Tewson and Chinnoks, a company with venerable roots and an awful name. After several aberrations trying to come up with a catchy name, the company settled on "DTZ Debenham Tie Leung". I hope they didn't overpay their name consultant!

The naming exercise wasn't Anthony's doing. Richard Lay, his former chairman was still laboring with the misconception that the sun had yet to set on the British Empire, and that a fine high quality old English name like Debenham must never be forgotten. I am being facetious though. Chairman Richard made up for any personal shortcomings he may have had in vision by being as fast on his feet as any man I have met. He was suave, good looking and a talker par excellence. No doubt women admired Richard more readily than men, but even taking advantage of this obvious asset, his real strength was his contributions to the business community in the UK. This recently earned him a CBE (Companion of the British Empire) just a step down from knighthood.

I did say Anthony was very English—and very intelligent. He would often answer a question with a quote from Shakespeare, Chaucer, Disraeli or Churchill, never blinking an eye that this might be out of his listeners' ordinary chain of conversation. He had been educated in English public schools and Christ Church College at Oxford, which he, and many others, considered the finest learning institution in Britain. He on occasion stated that Christ Church (the locals always skipped the "College") produced more prime ministers than any other college in the land. I did suggest to Anthony once, that the Reading Gaol might have given it a run for its money. Anthony read the law at Oxford, a profession that still enjoys a fine reputation in Britain. Actually, the lawyer joke is unknown in Britain; same stories are told, just relabeled accountant jokes!

While the Turnbulls' careers took them to the Greater London area, their first love was Beachfield, the old family summerhouse on the Isle of Wight. The Isle of Wight is a microcosm of southern England sitting just off the southern coast and guarding Portsmouth, the Royal Navy's largest base and Southampton, it's largest port. It can be reached from the mainland by plane, hydrofoil or car ferry with the longest voyage taking less than an hour. Once there you find lots of contrast: fishing ports, empty downs (downs are actually ups, or highlands) tourist traps, picturesque villages, ubiquitous row houses and one of the largest prison complexes in the U.K. Prominent also is Osborne House, Queen Victoria's vacation home (they call it a house but believe me, anywhere else it would be a mansion) where she had her little trysts with Mister Brown. Best of all, the Isle of Wight has endless vistas and some audaciously beautiful terrain.

Beachfield has three acres or so behind walls above the beach very near the center of Sandown, a slightly tired middle class resort on the east coast of the island. Beachfield was definitely not rundown, as the Turnbulls had turned their financial and creative attention to reviving this 12 bedroom, 6-bath sprawler that had fallen into disuse over the years after World War II. The family took up residence there during the London blitz. It faces a distant thus invisible Normandy on the French coast over a hundred miles to the east. Anthony remembers a clear dark night in 1944 when, from the cliff, he could see the faint flashes of the salvos announcing the onset of D-Day in far-off France.

Unlike Osborne House, Beachfield is not a mansion. It is a warm, well-used dwelling with well-kept grounds and an expansive view. When Anthony decided to retire, it was necessary to bring the house to a level of livability that the Turnbulls and their many guests could enjoy. The bathrooms were redone and the kitchen had a complete overhaul right down to an Aga, a mammoth Swedish made stainless steel oven that is the envy of any cook who has ever cast eyes upon it. The billiards room was refurbished with red velvet décor and Kew Gardens green wallpaper which sounds like bordello décor, but managed to come off extremely well. The common rooms were converted into comfortable havens as guests were expected to converse, exchange information and engage in verbal one-upmanship at all hours.

Seemingly, Beachfield is always open to guests. Weekends and holidays were especially busy at the house, as the Turnbulls spent part of each week in London. Company would straggle in all weekend. The guests were varied and versatile and as different as paper and rock. Anthony and Petronel have an uncanny way of selecting people that are compatible with each other. A hog farmer with a stud farm in Hampshire might be in deep conversation with a stylish television personality from BBC who had become a national persona because of her garden show; a dapper septagenerian driving a little Honda while escorting his new girl friend would arrive ten minutes before the financial baron in his Bentley; or a barrister from London, a Queen's Messenger from Surrey, a doctor from the Thames Valley and at least a dozen of our own family and friends would be engaged in deep conversation.

Cocktails were always served in the drawing room in anticipation of dinner prepared by Petronel (without domestic help) on her Aga. Occasionally Anthony would drive to the tiny port of Bembridge to buy fresh "bugs" from a local lobster fisherman. The entire basis of the weekend was conversation. Conversation before dinner, conversation during dinner, conversation during snooker and conversation over cognacs after dinner. Only at the breakfast table did the dialogues diminish. Anthony would wander down the street to the local news agent and return with *The Times,*

PETER MARR

The Telegraph, The Guardian, The Sun and a half a dozen other papers of various quality. In essence, this was the one time you prepared for the conversations held later in the day.

These visits were completely memorable. Jaundiced friends of mine, enjoying spectacular voyages through Britain and the continent, always came back and said: "That weekend at the Turnbulls was the highlight of our trip". It was definitely a highlight of ours as well.

I miss England. I think of it often. I mentally wander the streets and parks of London, and the annual visits back are all too short. It's not the same. I miss the people. I was happy there.

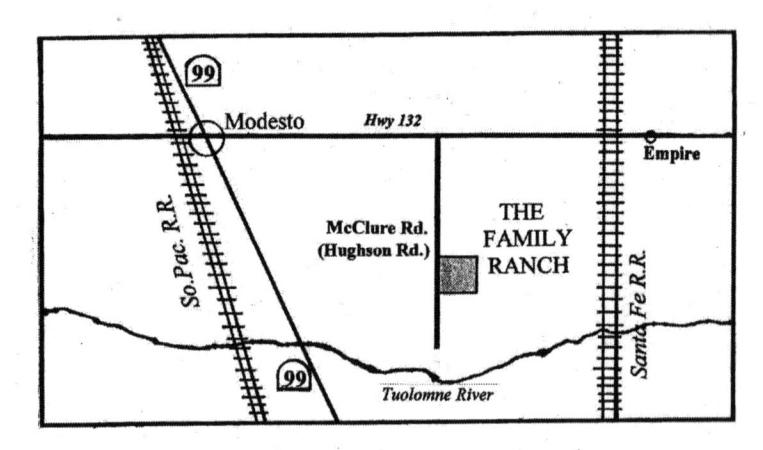

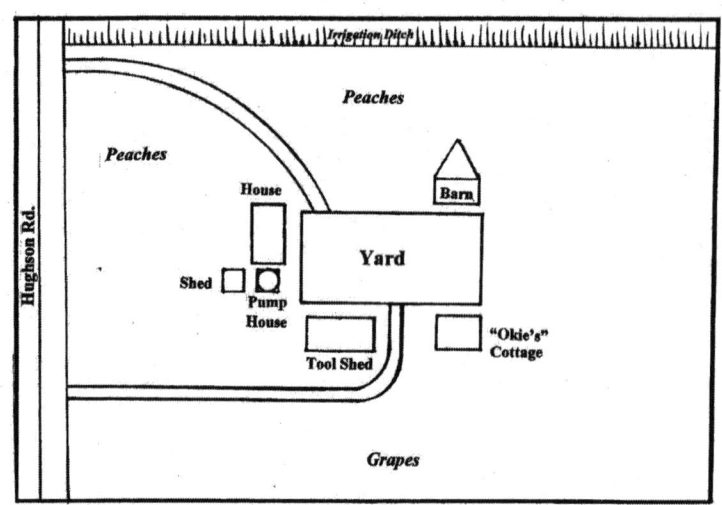

THE RANCH

Map 1

- Hwy 99
- Modesto
- Hwy 132
- Empire
- So. Pac. R.R.
- McClure Rd. (Hughson Rd.)
- THE FAMILY RANCH
- Santa Fe R.R.
- Tuolomne River

Map 2

- Irrigation Ditch
- Peaches
- Peaches
- Hughson Rd.
- House
- Shed
- Pump House
- Barn
- Yard
- Tool Shed
- "Okie's" Cottage
- Grapes

"The small towns stretched endlessly as you plied your way up the valley. Delano, Kingburg, Madera and Turlock with bigger towns like Bakersfield and Fresno to link them together"

THE RANCH

A PASTORAL CHILDHOOD

The ranch was four miles east of Modesto in California's great Central Valley. Many call it the San Joaquin Valley, but in reality that only refers to the southern half of it. The ranch sat a mile south of State Highway 132 just off a narrow agricultural lane called Hughson Road. It was a spread of 60 acres planted out in Elberta peaches, Thompson seedless grapes and apricots. Located on a bench above the Tuolumne River it was deep soiled having been the beneficiary of thousands of years of sediment buildup from the river. At its source in the Sierras, the Tuolumne was a wild stream, but having reached the valley floor it was lazy and sedentary. Just downstream, adjacent to Modesto was the home ranch of Ernest and Julio Gallo who popularized inexpensive wines in America. As successful as the Gallos had been, they remained remote from the Modesto community. They could, however, take fiscal pleasure from the success of their product, some of which like Thunderbird was drinkable only by derelict men suffering from third stage DT's.

The ranch belonged to my maternal grandmother, Myrtie Conneau

THE RANCH

Langdon. Myrtie was a story in herself. She was one of six children of French and Irish parents who had immigrated to Modesto in the 1860's. When her stone-mason father died prematurely, her mother, Annie Waters Conneau of County Sligo, sold the house and some rental cribs near the train tracks and reinvested the funds in a boarding house in Palo Alto. There she enrolled her two brightest children, one of whom was Myrtie, in a new local institution, Stanford University, only 10 years old at the time. Myrtie graduated in 1899 (just attending was quite an accomplishment for a woman in those days) and soon returned to her Modesto roots as a new school marm. The town banker, a widower by the name of Oral McHenry, soon spotted Myrtie, married her, fathered a son Merl, and died only three years later leaving her a comfortable inheritance. Soon after, she married a fellow schoolteacher, William Langdon. Both were bright and ambitious, and he found time to get a law degree before embarking on a career that ultimately led to positions as Superintendent of Schools for San Francisco, District Attorney of San Francisco and finally an appointment to the Supreme Court of the State of California. Not bad for a country schoolteacher!

The Langdons were not farmers, so the ranch, part of the legacy from Oral McHenry, was always leased to agricultural companies. These firms planted, managed, maintained and harvested the vineyards and orchards. They even allowed me to pick fruit and occasionally drive a tractor. The tractor privilege ended abruptly when I inadvertently demolished a young peach tree. The Ag firm master-leased the adjoining single bedroom cottage and subleased it out. Invariably, the cottage tenant was an impoverished itinerate farmer, or Okie, one of that body who have played such a key role in the Great Central Valley, and were depicted so graphically by John Steinbeck in his classic *The Grapes of Wrath*. As a very young boy, Sal and Pete, the barn's in-residence mules, enthralled me. Sal and Pete were not necessarily friendly, but to me, they were creatures bigger than life. One of my first inklings of sex was asking my parents just what those funny horses were doing stuck together like that. Even today I remain somewhat mystified by mules and how sterility could be the end result of the handiwork of a virile male and a fertile female.

PETER MARR

To find the ranch, you drove a mile south on Hughson Road from the Modesto-Empire highway, turned east onto an unpaved entry drive and passed through peach orchards for 100 yards before arriving in a large rectangular dirt courtyard. On your immediate right, forming one side of the courtyard, was the red two-story ranch house with its adjoining tank house. Straight ahead was a maintenance shed, then the one bedroom cottage and finally, an old barn on the left. The house was well gardened and set off nicely by large elms and poplars. Even more important to my brother Mike and I, was a mammoth fig tree next to the tank house and a fertile cherry tree across the road. We fought the birds for the sweet cherries in early summer and for the big plump figs in the fall. The ranch complex was imposing for that part of the country and stood like a sentry among the neat symmetrical rows of orchards and vineyards.

My first memory of the ranch was driving there from Los Angeles shortly before the outbreak of World War II. The eight-hour drive was an adventure for me and Mike (younger brother Bill was still too young to remember), especially navigating the narrow twisting Grapevine that plunged down from the Tehachapi Mountains to meet the very southern edge of the Great Valley. In 1940 it was a twisting two-lane road—today it is Interstate 5 with four lanes of traffic in each direction. We were especially proud of the Grapevine, as our parents always reminded us that that Uncle Jack Haviland had been an engineer on this job, one of the biggest highway projects ever.

The long drive north through the valley on Highway 99 was fascinating. Even though we may not have appreciated it, the road represented a great crosscut of Americana. The valley is perhaps the most fertile spot on earth with alluvial soils of great depth and plenty of snow water from the western flanks of the adjacent Sierra Nevadas. We soon were taught to identify cotton and alfalfa, how to distinguish a peach tree from an orange tree and learned the names of the great variety of animals we witnessed along the roadside. The first memorable landmark we would pass was the

THE RANCH

Lebec Hotel at the top of the Grapevine, followed by the Bakersfield Hotel arch, still in place over Highway 99. We always anticipated a stop at the Big Orange (a hideous looking sphere near Tulare that sold wonderful chilled fresh orange juice) and the drive-in restaurant in Madera, just north of Fresno. With three little boys in the car, our parents were obviously relieved to stop anywhere to attempt to regain a little sanity.

Generally the highway was two lanes although certain busy sections had been expanded to three-lane sections. These were the most dangerous types of road, as the center lane was a passing lane open to whoever got there first. The results were sometimes horrifying, and I can remember one time when our parents warned, "Don't look children!" so that we might not experience carnage that could have left us with endless evenings of nightmares.

We always searched for the series of Burma Shave placards that flanked the roadsides. These consisted of a half a dozen signs spaced a hundred feet apart. Sadly, these became one of the few casualties of the mostly beneficial 1965 Highway Beautification Act. In his marvelous book on the history of the English language, *Mother Tongue*, Bill Bryson chronicles several Burma Shave signs including:

> Don't take a curve / at 60 per / we hate to lose / a customer /
> BURMA SHAVE

Or another that was deemed too risqué in that more puritanical time:

> If wifey shuns / your fond embrace / don't shoot / the iceman /
> feel your face / BURMA SHAVE

The small towns stretched endlessly as you plied your way up the valley: Delano, Kingsburg, Madera and Turlock with small cities like Bakersfield and Fresno to link them together. Many of these hamlets had been settled through the efforts of the Southern Pacific Railroad, which, after the California gold rush, offered low prices for the land they had been granted by the government for building the railroads in the first place. Most of these grants were "checker boarded", as a result of the railroads having received alternate 640-acre sections over vast amounts of country. Magnanimously, the railroad then jacked up their transportation fees (the farmer had to get his product to market after all) and left the farmers on the brink of destitution. These events are described in detail in Frank Norris's classic, *The Octopus*.

I was to become much better acquainted with the ranch. My father had been an officer in the Navy since shortly after Pearl Harbor. He felt that tours of desk duty in Los Angeles and Philadelphia just weren't the contribution he wanted to make to the war. For over two years, he had pulled every string he could to get assigned to combat duty but to no avail. Finally he got his wish, and in 1944, he became the deck officer coordinating amphibious landings on the USS Winged Arrow, a troopship then in the Philippines but destined to proceed to Iwo Jima and Okinawa. My father's last stateside task was driving the family (Mother and the three boys) cross-country from Philadelphia to Modesto in a '39 Ford. It was an adventure for us but even more so for Dad as the car averaged two flats per day. My most specific memories of that trip were of Dad changing tires on the roadside in the Indiana countryside, next to an Oklahoma farm and at high noon in the scorching desert near Wickenburg, Arizona. Wartime tires were synthetic, not designed for cross-country travel and gasoline was available only through ration cards (the Navy had provided them in abundance to get us across the country) or the more nefarious offerings of the black market.

Upon our arrival on the west coast, we were ensconced for the duration of the war with Grandmother Myrtie and her younger widowed sister, Lena. With my mother, now pregnant with her fourth child, a daughter, Hilarie, it was definitely a matriarchal medley. As energetic as they were, they had close to a full time job overseeing three young boys, all of us under 10. Aunt Lena was a saint whose husband George had been a well-disguised rogue. George was the accountant for the family trust who, to afford his mistress, embezzled from the trust. Confronted by Myrtie's son, Merl, he

THE RANCH

stuck a hose in the tail pipe of his DeSoto and while his sudden earthly departure may have left the world a slightly better place, it wasn't any easier on Lena. She became a companion first to Myrtie and later to my mother, lived into her nineties and spread happiness to those that were fortunate enough to come into her sphere.

The Central Valley was a polyglot of cultures with Basque shepherds in Bakersfield, Dutch dairymen in Delano and the country's largest Armenian population in Fresno. Adding to the mélange were Mennonites and Dunkards, strict religious sects from Russia, Canada and other exotic spots. They usually kept to themselves but the men often hired out for farm work and the wives worked as domestics, always dressed in bonnets and gingham dresses and always devoid of make-up. Later, the Latinos were to become the workingman's backbone of the valley but in the thirties and forties, "the Okies", farmers driven from the plains by the dust storms and depression of the thirties, filled that function.

The Okies had overwhelmed this part of the valley. Our friends and most of our schoolmates at Empire Union Grammar School were Okies. They had wonderful names like Melvin Vessels, Clovis Hedley, and Alice Greenhill. It was Ted Langford however, that became our almost constant companion. He lived with his "Ma and Pa" in the cottage on the ranch and had arrived several years earlier when the family lost their small farm in western Oklahoma. Ted was about 13 and a big, big boy—well over 200 pounds. He was a lonely boy having been ridiculed by his peers for his size and seemed to feel more comfortable in the company of non-threatening younger boys like Mike and me. He was truly a gentle giant, and we were flattered by his attention.

We could walk the mile up to the highway to catch the school bus but it was much more adventuresome to trudge the two miles cross country tracking through stream beds, past barns, down rows of vineyards and orchards and skirting an occasional copse that might house a colony of hobos. This route to school was much more fun.

PETER MARR

School was school but we had a little incident to live down for some time before Mike and I gained the approval of our new peer group. My mother, I think with well meaning intent (she was always well meaning but this incident stretched her credibility) had sent us off to our first day at Empire Union Grammar school dressed in our recently acquired eastern finery from Philadelphia where Dad's Navy duty had taken us for a year. This garb included knickers, which were a de rigueur method of dress in Pennsylvania but generated only guffaws and worse at Empire. By the time Mike and I arrived home that first day, we had experienced fights at both recesses and lunch and only missed an after-school tussle by beating a hasty retreat home. Mother was a fabulous woman, but she got us blindsided on that one.

This matriarchal life was quite pleasant for us three young boys. The women were more than self-sufficient—if maintenance work became too physical or technical, a kindly Englishman from Modesto, Mr. Hampshire, was available to fix anything. The woodpeckers relished the wood siding of the ranch house and any of those birds that had the temerity to attack, received a blast from the in-house 30-ought-six. The adjoining tank house, a three-story structure with internal ladders housed the home's water supply and was out of bounds to us due to a proliferation of black widow spiders. I never saw one of these little terrors, but Mike and I were frightened enough of the thought to give the tank house a wide berth. Perhaps that was the ladies' way of keeping us from scaling its interior.

Summers were both hot and mosquito infested, not a pretty combination, but the porches were screened and with eastern exposures keeping the baking afternoon's sun at bay, the porches were the coolest spots to have dinner. After dinner we would often retire to the living room where we would surround the big Atwater-Kent stand-up radio to listen to our favorite radio shows of the day; *The FBI in Peace and War, Inner Sanctum* or *The Green Hornet*—featuring Bret Reid and his trusty servant, Kato. Radio was a bigger factor in our lives then than television is today. Saturday mornings were *Let's Pretend* with Smilin' Ed McConnell and its ever-present sponsor, Cream of Wheat, and each weekday at 5:00 would be the serial *Jack Armstrong, the All American Boy,* immediately followed by *Captain Midnight.* Of impact to the entire family was the nightly news. Newspapers in the Central Valley were especially "rural" and home delivery was not an option, so the war was followed through the radio. Gabriel Heater ranted and raved from New York (punctuated by his ever-present telegraph key) but Edward R. Murrow, Lowell Thomas and H.B Kaltenborn reported from London or Cairo and could bring the fronts alive. My mother knew Dad was in the Philippines and listened closest to the reports from the South Pacific, but we boys thought Dad was immortal and never took notice of Mother's quiet concern. We either were too self-centered or totally naïve about our father's mortality, but our innocence was rewarded as the war ended and he did come home. In the fall of 1945, he disembarked from his ship in Portland and took the train south to California. I can still remember my excitement and for some unknown reason, a touch of angst, as Mike and I raced the length of the Berkeley train station to jump into his arms and again experience the feeling of being a family.

While Modesto was only four miles away, visiting it from the ranch was a treat for us. During World War II, it was a town of 15,000, but today has grown to 180,000 and lost its rural appeal. It was an agricultural town that had a prosperous and well-defined central business district, its ultimate decay yet to be completed by the competition of shopping centers and Wal-Mart stores on the town's periphery. Modesto also served as the county seat for Stanislaus County. Its residential areas were lined with shade trees giving the neighborhoods a soft and inviting demeanor. Modesto had three theaters and countless churches, a high school and junior college and a minor league baseball team. It had three small hospitals, an airport, a Sears and a "Monkey Wards" store and, unknown to us at the time, a red light district down by the tracks. Often our trips to town were for a football game—the high school played Friday nights and the junior college on Saturdays. The town's most notable football export had matriculated to the College of the Pacific in Stockton where he played for America's oldest coach, Amos Alonzo Stagg. His name was unforgettable: Johnny Podesto from Modesto!

PETER MARR

Haircuts were still twenty-five cents (at least for a 10 year old) while a kid's ticket at the movies for the main feature and the weekly serial episode of Tom Mix or Ken Maynard came to all of twenty cents. A hardback copy of the latest potboiler about the adventures of Dave Dawson (spellbinder books that I never got too much of) was thirty cents and tamales at the little Mexican cocina near the Gallo plant were ten cents each.

To me the most exciting event in Modesto was the daily arrival and departure of the Southern Pacific's Valley Daylight, which journeyed from San Francisco down the length of the Great Valley and skirted the Tehachapis into Los Angeles. You could hear it at a distance as it approached town from the north splitting the air with its blaring whistle before its arrival was announced by a cacophony of noises: the hissing of steam, a metallic click as it passed over rail junctions and the almost frantic ring of the bells at the grade crossings where cross town traffic on G and H Streets waited patiently for the train's departure before they could cross. As it slowed to a stop, the rods of the engine seemed of sequoia stature and the wheels bigger than a small carnival's Ferris Wheel. The pistons expelled a gigantic hiss of steam as this Goliath appropriately came to its stop directly across from the arched sign spanning Highway 99 in the town's very heart. Its message read; "Modesto: Water, Wealth, Contentment, Health".

In five minutes, the Daylight was ready to roll again. No dallying, it was the most important train in the state, and you sensed that it knew it. The conductors almost hissed their stentorian calls of "All Aboard", the engine again expelled steam and the huge piston rods laboriously began to revolve. In order to warn traffic on B Street ahead, it blew its earsplitting whistle, which always seemed to startle us and left us with hearts pounding and feeling slightly out of breath. Like a large dog, waking from a nap and stretching in the sun, the Daylight pulled from the station, gained speed as it cleared the railroad bridge across the Tuolumne and soon faded from view. The ritual was always repeated and I never tired of it. My first solo train trip, a voyage on the Daylight to Los Angeles at age 10, still rates as one of the biggest adventures of my life.

A number of years ago, I returned to Modesto and took that opportunity to renew my memories of the ranch. As I headed east on Highway 132, I saw lots of new housing tracts, industrial parks and shopping centers and had some difficulty spotting the landmark of the Greenhill ranch at Hughson Road. I couldn't find a Hughson Road, but I did locate a McClure Road that had to be its successor. Such fleeting fame for the now unheralded Mr. Hughson! I headed down this former country lane where I had once walked to school with dense tule fog reaching to my waist with the sky blue above my shoulders and keeping my bearings by staying equidistant from the tops of the fruit trees lining the road. But now, huge industrial buildings had replaced the trees and vineyards. All the greenery was gone and the countryside had changed from its former sylvan softness to acres of concrete tilt-up walls devoid of trees and grass, just stacks of palettes strewn over asphalt yards. There were no ranch houses! When I reached the end of the road on the bluff above the Tuolumne River, I knew I had gone too far. I backtracked looking for anything familiar until, in the area I sensed the ranch should have been, I noticed a standing water pipe, a remnant of the irrigation ditch where Mike and I had escaped the heat and mosquitoes on many a sweltering summer day. Gone was the ditch, gone was the entrance road and gone was the ranch: Only this stupid standing water pipe remained.

The sinking sensation in my stomach hit bottom. The ranch truly was gone and my vision of it was now only a memory. Had I found it intact, it might have fallen into disrepair or have become so gentrified it would have been unrecognizable. If, by some small chance, it had looked the same with the zinnias and dahlias blooming and the mosquitoes buzzing, it would have tested credulity. Life is about change and things are meant to change; some for the better, some like this for the worse. What I had received was not my first lesson in change but certainly one of the most jolting. My memories of this wonderful old sanctuary will have to suffice.

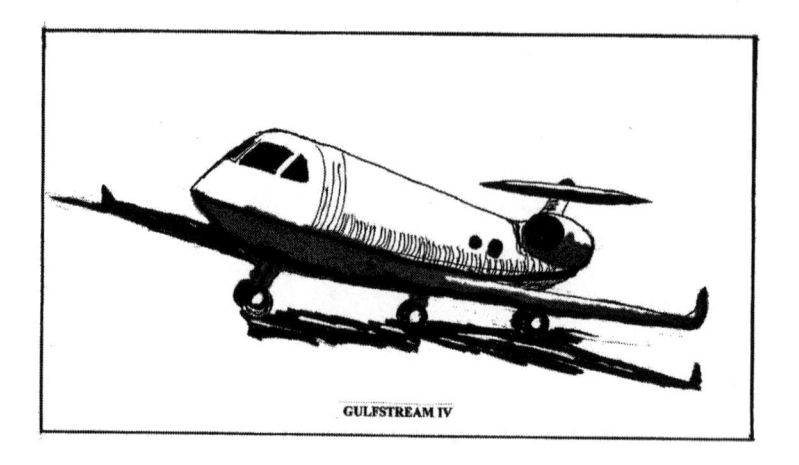

COSTA RICA

GULFSTREAM IV

"San Jose had a clean if
unimaginative city scape
surrounded by
striking mountains and a
sky dominated by the
constant movement
of clouds with
ever changing colors"

COSTA RICA

THE BIG GUY

Pat Cutbirth is a big guy. For starters, his neck measures 22 inches and he buys his shirts at Turnbull & Asser in London for a cool 150 quid a copy. He has an excuse; after all, the Gap or even Nordstrom isn't likely to provide shirts off the rack for a 22-inch neck!

Pat is from Bakersfield in the Central Valley of California. Now Bakersfield is sort of like Denver; great backdrop, but sitting on a pretty shitty platform. Denver is fairly plain Jane but has the Rockies soaring above it for aesthetic relief. Dusty intemperate Bakersfield enjoys the same grandeur, but in this case, it has the majestic Sierra Nevadas in its backyard. The town made it from oil and row crops, neither of which is particularly attractive, and it has to be the most unappealing of the valley towns, hardly a stellar group themselves. Bakersfield is famous for the people who have left rather than stayed—Merle Haggard and Frank Gifford come immediately to mind. I am constantly running into successful people elsewhere who have forsaken their Bakersfield roots.

Pat was dating my daughter Kaelyn and enjoying the good life more readily available on the San Diego coast than in Bakersfield. He liked the best whiskey, food and wines and traveled on a first class standard when some might have felt he only justified a beer budget. He did it with a certain amount of aplomb however. Kaelyn had joined Pat and Mark Scudder in an aircraft management business, which in addition to managing rich folks' aircraft, hoped to generate a profit brokering corporate jets to movie and recording stars and the proliferation of new multi-millionaires and billionaires that had been nurtured in California by the Information Revolution. Pat felt very comfortable with these groups. He was able to keep his bullshit quotient under enough control so that his encyclopedic knowledge about aircraft imbued a confidence in his buyers that Pat was the right guy to find them the right airplane. Underneath this thin veneer of sophistication, he is a promoter at heart, which made Pat's life both unpredictable and mercurial.

Three days before Christmas, Pat mentioned to me that he had a "demo flight" on a Gulfstream IV flying down to Costa Rica in Central America the day after Christmas. It would return after the first of the year. Demo flights, as I was to find out, were the method that major corporate jet manufacturers showcased their planes to qualified users at cut-rate prices in the hopes of selling them an aircraft. This was one of Pat's great come-ons to his clients. Where the flights went was left to the discretion of the client, so one of the perks he regularly received was being able to accompany the prospect to some exotic spot. You could be sure that the manufacturer had a rep along for the trip as well. Those poor over-traveled souls were there to extol the virtues of Gulfstream, Falcon, Cessna or whoever and usually had to deadhead home the following day. In any case, I readily agreed to join Pat and his partner, Mark, as the "extra freeloader." Though I had heard great things of Costa Rica, I had never seen it, and of course my head was turned by the prospect of a private trip on a Gulfstream. I had been on corporate jets a number of times, and what was not to like?

Pat had Rich Sulpizio, the president of Qualcomm, a major wireless technology operation, in tow for a demo flight to San Jose. That is not the San Jose in Silicone Valley, but the capitol in Costa Rica. Pat had arranged yet another demo for a Falcon jet that would return Rich and his wife Gabby to San Diego after the end of their ten-day vacation. That was to be our means of transportation home as well.

Sulpizio was used to traveling on corporate jets as they were part of the Qualcomm culture, but even he seemed taken aback by the smoothness and opulence of the Gulf Stream. This is a 35 million dollar aircraft, and the finishing touches are better than you would find in a Beverly Hills estate that had been decorated by Hank Morgan. Natural woods, plush carpeting, leather seats that swivel in any direction and also convert to beds and two loos! All of this along with a flight attendant and catered meals for the seven of us aboard who only half filled the aircraft. I doubt that Sulpizio bought that plane, but I know he enjoyed the flight.

Our pilots were on their maiden voyage to San Jose, and after a late evening landing, we were primed for the typical VIP treatment upon arrival. I don't know what we expected (previously San Diego had provided limos, porters and a real honest to goodness red carpet), but being ferried from the plane to the Immigration Hall in a truck that had experienced at least twenty years combating Costa Rica's notorious potholes was an inauspicious start. Late at night, all Immigration Halls seem the same. Confusion abounds in darkness, odors are accentuated and the emptiness of a large hall makes it both dreary and morose. San Jose was no exception and the VIP treatment consisted of a single tired agent with his head bowed, thumbing through our passports until he had satisfied himself that this group was not going to do physical harm to his country. Pat, ever the salesman, assured Rich and his party that we were receiving special treatment, and Rich was good enough not to ask what standard handling might have been: the Spanish Inquisition?

Landing after dark at a new city always generates an uneasy feeling with me. There is no third dimension to a city in the dark; your sense of the place is only as deep as your narrow night vision permits, and any sense of direction you might possess is in shambles. Mountains and rivers are lost in the dark and only a manmade display such as a Manhattan skyline can help you put your new venue into logical order. It goes without saying, that San Jose lacked a New York skyline. What you see at night all changes when you see it for the first time in daylight. Daylight not only highlights the scars and splendors hidden by the dark, but with it comes the confusion of having been set down in a vacuum with no frame of reference of how you got there.

San Jose has a mellow cityscape surrounded by dramatic and striking mountains and a sky dominated by the constant movement of rapidly scurrying clouds with ever-changing colors. The city itself was clean if unimaginative. The fingers of coffee plantations encroach into the city much like the slums of the Brazilian favellas spill unwanted into their beautiful Rio. In San Jose, the plantations are beautiful trespassers, who welcome you with their softness and greenery.

Two days in Costa Rica hardly makes me an expert. It was long enough, however, to appreciate its beauty, vibrancy and the genuineness of its people. While the city couldn't be described as charming, it was interesting, clean and prosperous, a very complex mixture of the old and the new. You couldn't help but notice the differences as well as the similarities that existed between Costa Rica and its bigger and more diverse Latin American neighbor, Mexico. Unlike Mexico, where the populace never picks up anything, Costa Rica was clean. People seemed to take pride in cleaning up after themselves, and trash removal was provided three times a week. Most homes had a permanent wire sided basket for trash attached to the front of their house. They were used. Make no mistake though, for like Mexico, the culture is Hispanic and you are never very far removed from that special Latin ambience.

Security was evident everywhere and a number of homes, even in modest neighborhoods, had wrought iron spiked fences with spiraling concertina wire protecting the property. Many of the fancier homes in the Los Laureles district had, as in Mexico, professional guards. The justification given for all this security was Nicaragua! Their neighbor to the north is a very poor country, which went through a disastrous civil war over a decade ago. The war originated an exodus of their disadvantaged to Costa Rica and elsewhere. Today, up to a million Nicaraguans have pushed Costa Rica's population to near the 5 million mark. When the Nicaraguans first arrived, there were not enough jobs to go around and increased crime was the end result. Today, with prosperity, crime is down and the by-product is that the Nicaraguans are doing the work that Costa Ricans no longer want to do. Apparently they are now prospering without the need to burgle, but you don't know if this isn't a self-serving myth. Does the security threat still exist, or are all the safeguards not just vestiges of past dangers that now act as status symbols?

Another difference from Mexico is skin color as the Costa Ricans are white complexioned unlike most Mexicans whose color evidences their strong Indian heritage. Executives, tradesmen, cab drivers, waiters, and hookers—almost everyone we encountered was white. Of the Latin American countries I had visited, only Argentina also evidenced this anomaly. Perhaps this observation is not politically correct, but it is quite obvious and unusual for a Latin American nation.

During the next two days, we were able to wander the streets of San Jose, have a cocktail at a hillside replica of Scarlett O'Hara's Tara, drink coffee from a mountain plantation and peer into the aquamarine waters of a cloud reflected mountain lake nestled in the crater of an active volcano. In addition there were waterfalls, rain forests and an appealing rural countryside that epitomizes this small and friendly country. I was ready for more and wanted a chance to see the contrasting coastlines of the Caribbean and the Pacific, experience Costa Rica's invigorating river rafting and discover their seldom raining but always damp, Cloud Forests.

Pat was scheming again, and pressing business called him and Mark home two days into our scheduled eight day visit. I was given the option of staying by myself for another week and flying back on the Falcon, or returning the following day with Pat and Mark. Perhaps my spontaneity had left me, perhaps my spirit of adventure had departed in a mountaintop fall in New Zealand or a dirt bike accident in Baja, but I opted to return home. Maybe it was being away from home over a holiday or learning that all the good resorts were booked for the New Year and that a desultory chain hotel in San Jose (that could just as easily have been in Wichita) was to be my home for another week. I had lots of reasons, none necessarily good, and I got on the airplane feeling a little sheepish and a little disappointed in myself for doing so.

Pat is a master at weaving a story. Actually, he is full of more shit than a Christmas goose. The pressing business at home turned out to be another private jet opportunity to spend the New Year in Hawaii with client Glen Frey and the Eagles. Yeah, had I been Pat, I might have made the same decision, but the convoluted unraveling of his aims were in the best tradition of the CIA's top spymaster. I have yet to decide if he is amoral or an artist.

All was not lost. In the greater scheme of things, it was a nice little trip. I was able to see a new country and experience a different culture. I spent time with some interesting people and sampled the life style of the super wealthy on a very pampered flight. So either because of, or perhaps in spite of Pat's prowess as the consummate snake oil salesman, I gained a little insight, perhaps a touch of personal growth and added a jigsaw piece to my negligible, but hopefully expanding, grasp of the puzzle that is our wonderful and confusing world.

BAJA MOTORCYCLES

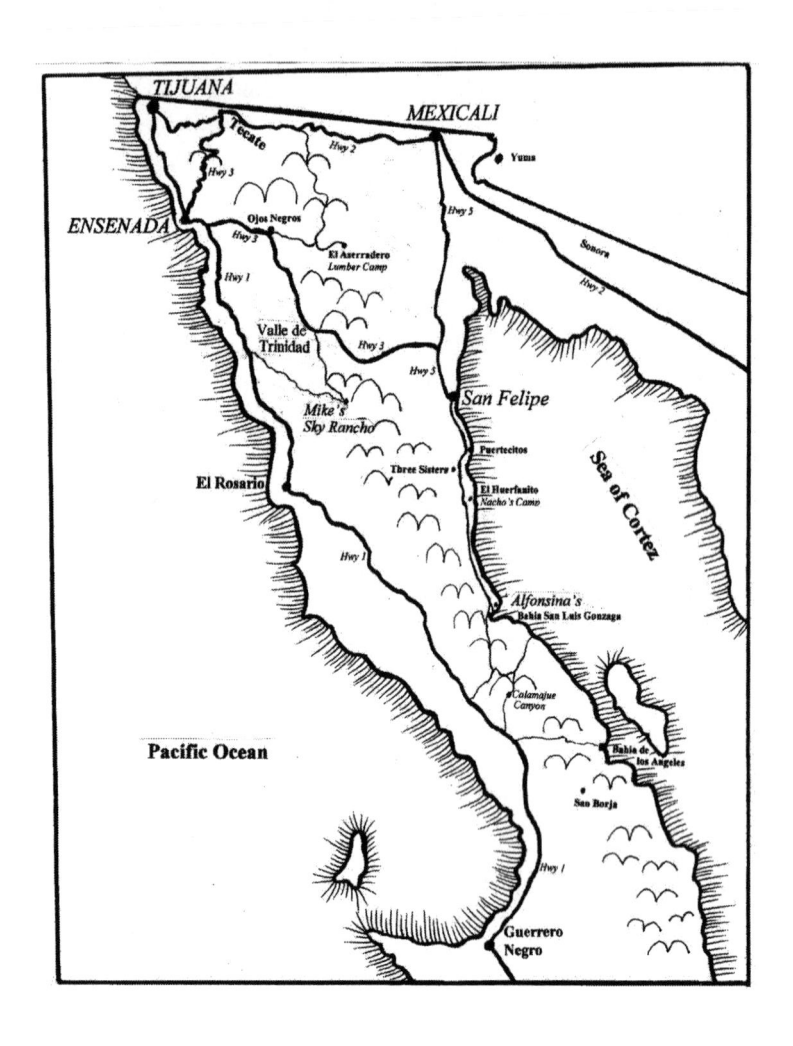

" Motorcycle riding is like roller coasters. You either love them or hate them"

BAJA AND MOTORCYCLES

THE LAST FRONTIER

What is it about motorcycles that so fascinate grown men? They truly generate terror in some while providing pure elation to others. Riding is like roller-coasters; there is no middle ground. You either love them or hate them.

While I am an advocate of motorcycles, it took a number of years before I experienced the elation of riding. You see, I had this conception that motorcycles were different than cars which you got into, turned the key and drove off. Motorcycles were machinery and needed lots of attention and lots of know-how. Being at least a part-time student of myself, I realized that things mechanical and Peter Marr had absolutely nothing in common. I am mechanically inept, and the intricacies of an engine (or for that matter, even a simplistic gadget) were as clear to me as advanced classical Greek. My friend, Dan Sweet, has had a long time love affair with speed, which he satisfies with motorcycles, fast boats and innocent looking passenger cars that he floor-boards at will. Dan assured me that, mechanically, the maintenance of motorcycles was a cinch, and, in any case, he would help me "keep up" the bike. Dan's enthusiasm for all things fun resulted in his toying with the truth at times. If motorcycle maintenance was so simple, why was his garage covered with so many disjointed parts that it was a challenge to park his cars or even hang up his garden tools?

To me, the speed factor that motorcycles offered was only ancillary to the opportunity they brought to explore the last frontier of California, the astounding peninsular deserts of Mexico's Baja California. Visions of this land had enthralled me for years and all of a sudden, Dan gave me the push to realize these dreams and best of all, to take on a new challenge: motorcycles.

Baja California extends almost 1000 miles south of the U.S. border separating the Pacific from the Gulf of California, that splendid body of water the Mexicans refer to as the Sea of Cortez. First the Spaniards and later the Mexicans tried to conquer Baja's empty vastness but had only partially succeeded. Settlements were usually along the coast but always located where water could be tapped. After all, Baja really is a very arid extension of the Great Sonora Desert.

A spine of mountains runs the length of the peninsula reaching as high as 10,000 feet in the pine forests of the north. In its midriff, scattered farming and ranching communities such as San Ignacio cluster around springs and wells creating their almost incongruous patchworks of green surrounded by Baja's immeasurable stretches of arid harshness. Some of the small ports on the Sea of Cortez such as Loreto and Santa Rosalia ship ore and agricultural products to the mainland, and their fishing fleets keep the populace well supplied with basic ingredients for superb fish tacos, shellfish, and indigenous seafood. Even though the resorts of La Paz and Cabo San Lucas typify the south, the huge preponderance of people who vacation at the popular southern tip of Baja only see the peninsula in transit from 35,000 feet.

The Rookie

As I mentioned, my motorcycle advisor was Dan Sweet. My training grounds were the dry lakebeds of the Southern California's Mojave Desert.

PETER MARR

We would trailer our bikes to the Spanish Bit, a raunchy roadside beer joint near El Mirage Dry Lake bed in the Mojave Desert. There we would park, unload the bikes and hit the little trails that meandered through the desert's interior.

Now, Spanish Bit was a real study. The proprietors, a middle aged couple, obviously drank up all of their meager profits. The place was a throwback to the thirties, and I'm sure the premises hadn't been swept since then. As I remember, the hostess's name was Roxy or something like that. Over the years, she had accumulated both mileage and tonnage, but given enough suds and encouragement, she would remove her massive bra and go topless behind the bar. Very classy!

Buck Jones, an intense old friend of mine, rode with us at times. On his first visit to Spanish Bit he became desperate enough to have to use the only john in the establishment. Within 30 seconds of entering this room not much larger than a cabinet, he burst out with his trousers around his ankles, hollering and frantically waving his arms. He had heard a whirring noise, turned around and saw a coiled rattlesnake behind the commode!

My motorcycle lessons amounted to following Dan and imitating what he did—real basic "On the Job Training"! I rode his old two stroke Husquivarna that wailed like a banshee but was super quick. After two or three trips to the desert, Dan blessed me with the information that I was now qualified to go to Baja and I had to commit to acquiring a bike. I was so enthused that I went out and bought a new Yamaha TT500, the biggest stock off-road bike on the market. It had a 4-stroke engine, which allowed it to use regular gas, which was supposedly more dependable than the mixed-gas 2-strokes. As a result, most 2-strokes were a rarity in Baja.

The day finally arrived for my first Baja voyage. Four of us: Dan Sweet, Bill Ostrom, Bill Inglis and I trailered our bikes on the paved highway to San Felipe at the northern end of the Sea of Cortez some 150 miles below Mexicali. We planned the trip to last for five or six days.

These guys were all seasoned motorcyclists. Dan, a gifted athlete had been a top class sprinter at USC. On bikes, he ran third for a good portion of the famous Barstow to Vegas race before he hit a rock and broke his foot. Wiry and full of energy he never tired and had only one speed: full ahead. Bill Ostrom, amazingly still riding in his seventies, was also the wiry type. He was an insurance adjuster who worked with vehicles every day and was one of the best Baja mechanics I ever saw. Bill was the only one in our group who rode one of the finicky 2-strokes but he rode it beautifully and almost never fell. Bill Inglis was a tough stocky type, an Anglo raised in the Los Angeles barrio of Boyle Heights. While he had a genuine heart of gold, no one screwed with Bill.

On the first day we would follow a southerly route that followed the shoreline of the Sea of Cortez and finished in Gonzaga Bay. The second day we wandered inland from Gonzaga until coming back to the Sea of Cortez at Bahia de Los Angeles. After a day checking out the remote region south of the Bay of L.A., we would retrace our tracks back to San Felipe.

San Felipe is the closest port on the Sea of Cortez to the American border and is accessible from Mexicali by good road. The downtown used to have a modicum of charm, but competition for the low end American tourist dollar left the village with a back-street poverty and the downtown with a junk store veneer. Gone is Arnold's, the funky beachfront motel that was the only place an offroader would stay. T-shirt shops, shabby discos and cheap sidewalk taco stands have replaced it (buy at your own risk). There are new fancy resorts on the beach south of town but that is another world, not San Felipe. The Miramar Bar is still in the heart of town. One night we saw a drunken American take a swing at an armed policeman. We thought that if he lived he would be in jail for several years, but the federale must have had a senior moment as he chuckled, got him in a bear hug and ultimately released him to what must have been a monster hangover. Rueben's is a beachfront spot on the north edge of town where they once sold a kilo of cooked shrimp for two or three dollars, but a combination of inflation and the ever-present greed for the

American tourist dollar has reached Rueben's. The shrimp is now twenty dollars a kilo. To make matters worse, it lost the little ambience it did have by double-decking their beachfront tent sites!

Before leaving San Felipe, Dan warned me that, in anticipation of this trip, all of the bikes had been fitted with new knobby tires, and the roadbed to Puertocitos was straight and rocky. He said my fellow riders would try to take you by surprise and dive in your path, their new knobbies spraying you with small rocks. Heeding this warning and with butterflies in my stomach, I started south on a cool and sparkling fall morning. Dan was right about the roadbed which had a multitude of small rocks that were just pushed aside by the dirt bikes as they blasted through at 60-70 miles an hour. After about three miles, a streak passed on my left, cut in front of me and showered me with rocks. One rock was the size of a tennis ball and caught me right in the sternum literally doubling me over and taking my breath away. Guess what? It was Dan accentuating his resignation as my mentor and the installation of himself as a competitor!

South of the little sun-baked hamlet of Puertocitos the road turns into a narrow two-rutter, and we breathed easier after we had successfully traversed the sinister inclines of the infamous Three Sisters. The contrast of harsh desert and iridescent blue water is never more dramatic than on this coastline. Before turning inland the road dips into our first day's destination, Gonzaga Bay, a striking ten-mile crescent of undisturbed white sand beach. I almost cried when I read recently that this was one of the spots on the Baja coast that the Mexican government has chosen to develop as a tourist oriented yacht anchorage. *Qué lástima!* What a shame! There are two small hamlets on the north end of the bay, separated by a quarter of a mile boat ride, or four miles by road. Papa Hernandez's is the northern outpost and sits on the throat of a small cove. It is a fishing village that consists of a few shacks and a small *bodega* that at times sells cold beer and soft drinks. We generally kept our distance from Papa Hernandez' as it was junky, depressing and permeated with the stench of old fish. The only accommodations had spring beds without mattresses, which years later and in desperation, we had to use one night.

BAJA AND MOTORCYCLES

The southern village, Alfonsinas, is on a sand spit peninsula backed by a lagoon that sometimes floods the airstrip paralleling its flank. You definitely check the tide charts before you fly into this strip. It is a quarter mile of small beach cottages on land leases to American pilots or fishermen who use them for part of the year. With the closest shopping at least a four-hour drive, you come well supplied when you arrive. Alfonsinas does have a small café and rents out modest but clean rooms. The proprietors trade with the shrimpers that work that part of the coastline for their freshly caught shellfish, usually bartering whisky or beer. The dinners on a patio cantilevered over the beach put anything else north of La Paz to shame. It has to be the closest thing to Wolfgang Pucks in the back coumtry.

The following day the two-rutter dirt road led us inland through the dramatic Calmajue Canyon. Almost magically, a tiny stream germinates soft green grasses during its four-mile life before vanishing in the dry fields of sage at its mouth. This primitive road weaves through the almost indiscernible ruins of an old mission, cactus fields of ocotillo, cholla and saguaro and through magnificent gardens of lurking boulders. We spied herds of sheep tended by lone Basque shepherds living in primitive trailers. God knows how they got the trailers or themselves to such a remote spot. I am told that these nomads, who migrated from the Pyrenees and recognize no national boundaries, frequent the mountains all the way into California's Sierra Nevadas.

Prior to reaching a short stretch of the trans-peninsular highway, we crossed Laguna Chapala on a faint track. The lakebed is like talcum and more than one motorcycle or truck has mired down in this powdery quicksand. Our destination, Bahia de Los Angeles affectionately called the Bay of L.A. is connected by paved road to the trans-peninsular highway, but the macadam stopped several miles from town enabling one to enter town majestically in swirls of dust. The Mexican contractors must have run out of money as they neared the Bay of L.A., so they shifted their attention to the little settlement and paved the section through town.

For several years now, the Bay of L.A. has had a motel with a decent restaurant and, believe it or not, a swimming pool. After its construction, the swimming pool alone was enough of a reason to make us customers, as upon arrival, we enjoyed being pampered with a poolside margarita on a sweltering afternoon. On this first trip, the only lodgings in town were at Mama Diaz's. Mama Diaz was a matriarch with a rasty disposition. Should she not like the way someone looked or acted, she told him to find different lodgings, a difficult task since, for a long time, she had the "only game in town". Incidentally, if there was a Papa Diaz, I never saw him or he must have been invisible.

On this vast and dramatically empty bay, Mama Diaz had managed to site all the rooms so no one had a view of the water. Instead the rooms faced the interior airstrip putting you in danger of errant Cessnas and only providing you with a view of its beautiful bay through the slit window in your bathroom. Dan suggested a ride along the beach out to the sand spit peninsula dividing the inner and outer bays. It seemed a magnificent idea, and we had a spirited ride around the arc of the bay to the point at the end of the peninsula. Most parts of the Sea of Cortez are subject to substantial tidal action but at the time, the bay was at low tide. Seeing this Dan said, "Hey the tide is out, let's cut straight across the sea bed back to Mama Diaz's and save some time." I nodded my head in enthusiastic agreement. Not a good decision. As we reached the middle, the muck got deeper and deeper and we sunk in over our rims. The mud flats made us sweat it every foot of the way and only running our big husky 4-stroke engines at full throttle got us across, otherwise the bikes would now be part of a marine monument and this chapter finished.

Mama Diaz served turtle steak when it was still ecologically correct to do so. Turtle steak, like rattlesnake, alligator and ostrich, is supposed to taste like chicken. I find it difficult to make this comparison, but if it makes the tree huggers any happier, I know turtle steak will never replace Chicken Kiev. Of course it is now banned, so the question is moot. Being one of the few places we knew where you could get turtle steak basted in beer, we always ordered it.

Mama Diaz had a simpleton teen-age son for whom she had bought a Mustang. All day he sat under the awnings in the yard polishing it. When dusk fell, he took to the road. He would rev up the engine and race on the paved road scattering urchins all the way from the tire repair shack where the asphalt started to the town's modest plaza, a town square without trees or grass. At that point he would turn the Mustang around, rev it again, peel rubber and race back to the tire repair shack. For hours he would do this, which not only tested his sanity but ours as well. So much for Saturday night fever at Bahia de los Angeles.

A devil wind would sometimes blow with a vengeance at the Bay of L.A. ruining all prospects for the fishermen. It made the anglers who had driven 12 hours from the border very testy. One especially crusty old fogy was complaining to us that he had been there a week while the wind blew and he couldn't fish. He was really aggravated. He turned his back on us to show off his T-shirt which had *"Pinche viento"*, printed on the back. He was a man of his convictions. *Pinche viento* means, fuck the wind.

We took a side trip from the bay to Mission San Borja located deep in the mountains in the middle of the peninsula. Like Father Serra's string of missions in Alta California, Baja has a number of mission outposts as well. While not necessarily as majestic as Santa Barbara or San Gabriel, these little missions are still tiny outposts of humanity in a harsh land. We reached San Borja by a very primitive road that featured erosion ruts the size of the Grand Canyon. I know this because I disappeared into one and wrestling the bike out was a major accomplishment. San Borja exists because it has water. At the time, there may have been fifty inhabitants in this hidden and attractive palm filled valley where irrigation channels connect fields of melons, squash and lettuce. The mission building is remarkably well preserved. The village is so small and remote that the priest only visits it monthly. Somehow the locals maintained the church in this tiny village too poor to even have a bodega.

While the return trip seems anti-climatical in my mind now, I know at the time it was as invigorating as was the first part of my maiden trek. I guess the rookie passed muster as I was asked back on the next trip. This was in spite of my having made ten "premature dismounts" during the five-day adventure. I told my pals that my inability to stay on the motorcycle was a result of my TT500's great torque in combination with the slippery decomposed granite surface. If the truth were known, I was in awe of Baja's breathtaking scenery. I quickly forgot the realities of "safety first" while absorbed in Baja's remarkable vistas.

MIKE'S SKY RANCH

Across the world, off-road fanatics view Mike's Sky Ranch as a motorcyclist's Valhalla. Mike's is buried in the Santa Rosa Mountains, 150 miles below the U.S. border and some 30 miles from the closest paved road. It rests in a cottonwood filled ravine that includes a Baja rarity, a 12-month running stream complete with trout, the San Rafael River. The white-stuccoed buildings forming the small complex sit on a ledge above this swath of greenery. From the patio in the evenings, you can visually pan the purple-hued mountains before spotting, halfway up the grade, the single alamo tree that turns a vivid yet soft yellow-green, a result of the sun hitting it just perfectly at that time of day. In the far distance you can catch the first faint purrs and the changing shift patterns of the four stroke engines and feel the sound vibrations slowly increase as the last motorcycle visitors of the day near the ranch. You reflect that, even with this subtle man-made intrusion, the earth seems terribly incongruously peaceful.

Mike Leon, who was an entrepreneur and Mexican motorcycle rider, put together the rancho well before my first visit. Several miles away, he built a modest landing strip for private planes giving the place its name: Mike's Sky Ranch. Mike was an outstanding motorcyclist but he tended to be a grouchy bastard, and his hostelry and culinary abilities might be considered suspect. Mike's pure touch of genius was to assure that the ranch served as a pit stop for the cars and motorcycles competing in the S.C.O.R.E Baja 500 (I'm still trying to figure out just what S.C.O.R.E means) and Baja 1000 which annually runs up and down the Baja peninsula. Most of the pit stops for these races are on desolate wind swept mesas or sited on scorching desert dry lake beds, thus Mike's, complete with cerveza, tequila, hot meals and warm beds, was a great favorite with the pit crews. Over time Mike's became an off-roaders' retreat, and the airport was abandoned. Interestingly, the aviators that still fly Baja and once frequented Mike's transferred their allegiance to the airstrip at the Mehling Ranch, 15 miles down a very bad road. Mrs. Mehling, who ran a very nice inn, would not allow motorcycles on her premises although she would allow a biker inside and serve him a cold cerveza or soft drink if he parked out of sight and minded his manners.

Mike passed away several years ago and his namesake son, young Mike, took over the Rancho. Mike, the son, has turned the place around even though it still might come up short when compared to a Motel 6. Luxury is not the reason we go there and its rustic nature is a major part of the charm and charisma that exist there.

The Valley de Trinidad is an hour north of Mike's. It is a big wide valley, bisected by a few long straight roads that run through large agricultural fields with windbreaks of tall eucalyptus sentinels acting as property demarcations. Most certainly, the roads are used at night by drug smugglers as airstrips. On its north edge is a grim and dusty town that has its own name but is always called Valley of Trinidad. Basically the town evolved from an *ejido*, a misguided result of Mexican land reform that tends to make a Mississippi sharecropper's habitat look luxurious. The road from Trinidad to Mike's is graded (we call them fire roads in the states) and a great dirt bike road. Some of my most inspired riding took place on that road, and Dan Sweet challenged me every time we rode it. The first few miles cross the Valle de Trinidad, which is flat-out riding country. There should be no surprises on these level roads but on one occasion, I had one. At 80mph, I hit an unanticipated dip in the road that was filled with a hidden overflow of irrigation water. All my body, save my arms, left the bike before I abruptly settled, askew and shaken, back on the seat never having lost an iota of speed. Later I found mud marks on my left knee, which had obviously touched the ground. I thanked the stars for reflexes I didn't know I had.

The next 20 miles of the road to Mike's traverses through the badlands: twisty, off-cambered roads that are a test of dexterity. Once Bill Inglis and I were really moving through those turns when we spied a stock Jeep Cherokee up ahead. He had seen us gaining on him, but surprisingly, instead of letting us catch and pass him, he let it rip. He not only pulled away from us but in a very short time was forever out of our sight. We were abashed at having a stock jeep make us look so bad. Upon arriving at Mike's, we saw the Jeep. At the bar we met its driver, Walker Evans. Evans it turns out has won absolutely every off road race invented. While we remained sheepish, we didn't feel quite as inadequate.

The last 8-10 miles of this road is over a five hundred foot ridge that finishes with a long downhill into the San Rafael River and then Mike's. Oh, what a wonderful road! After a few trips we knew all the corners, dips and swerves of the terrain and we took them at speeds above our ken. As we rose up its heights, we had to know the road, as the first half headed westward directly into a setting sun so brilliant that it virtually rendered us sightless. The sun be damned for the sun was at our back on the down slope. We would slide the corners, goose up the revs on the grades and smooth it around the tricky spots as we glided past that glimmering alamo tree. If Dan tried to pass, I "took no prisoners" and left no room and expected the same in return. At the very bottom of the hill was the ford that crossed the little San Rafael River. We had to be careful and cognizant of its water level, which varies substantially at different times of the year. If I hit it too fast, I threw up a wall of water that killed my engine and left me cursing and trying to kick start the bike in the middle of the stream. If I slowed down to nurse a lead, Dan would fly by and power up the last little slope into Mike's awaiting my arrival with a big grin of superiority on his face. What humiliation! God though, was that run a trip! I loved that finish!

As I remember, the interior of Mike's is, let's say, unusual. There is a pool table in the entry room but the only time I ever saw it in use was when Bill Inglis slept on it one cold night when the inn was full. The entire room is plastered with business cards from virtually anywhere you could imagine. Motorcycling has obviously changed a lot since the Hell's Angels era now that bikers have business cards! Off the entry room is both the bar and the kitchen/dining room. The bar is dark, leather padded and plastered with the same girly calendars you would see on a mechanic's wall. Added to the décor are S.C.O.R.E. T-shirts, hats coated with 40 weight and an occasional accelerator cable or foot peg. This is not a bar where you order a scotch and soda with a twist! The brand of cerveza is dependent upon what Mike trucked up from his weekly 200-mile supply run to Ensenada. Usually there is a choice of Modelo Negro or Pacifico. No complaints! Your choice of spirits is limited: tequila. No Herradura here. If you wanted tequila you are given something called Señor Paco or some such name, which has to be kerosene spiked with jalapeño pepper juice.

The long rectangular dining room is set up family style and each table is supplied with a regular assortment of condiments complete not only with salsa and Tabasco but also with incongruous containers of Wishbone Ranch and Thousand Island salad dressings. This has never changed. Dinner is simple. Salad with all the bottled dressing you want: tortillas, frijoles, a canned veggie, pork served on Friday and steak on Saturday. Bring your own jackhammer for the steak. With a lot of hungry dudes in attendance, there were very few leftovers. By the by, Mike's does get occasional "motorcycle molls," who while surrounded by men, have to wonder if these guys left their testosterone on their foot pegs. Where on this earth other than Leisure World could you discover that a guy's first topic isn't always women? Nowhere else I guess, for at Mike's: it's bikes.

The bikes are parked in an arcade that separates the swimming pool from the bluff that fronts the riverbed below. It is the best spot in the house. When Mike Senior ran the place, the pool had enough sludge on the top to support a dune buggy. I would rather have taken a dip in the La Brea Tar Pits. Young Mike (young, he must be approaching 50), amazingly and to his credit, cleaned up the pool and save being pretty damn cold, it is swimable. The real attraction is the motorcycle arcade, lined with all the parked dirt bikes as if it was a motorcycle dealership. There, at all hours, you will find their owners tinkering and discussing the relative merits of their machines. Then, the Hondas followed by the Yamahas were in favor, but there were always a few exotic ATK's or KTM's although few had the slightest idea what those acronyms stood for.

With few exceptions, the riders are mechanically clever and adaptive. Once Bill Ostrom rebuilt a clutch that had burned out in the middle of the forest, miles from help. Bill disassembled it to find the cork, which lined the clutch pads, had burned off. He sent the entire group off to find the right kind of rock to scrape the pads and give them a rough finish that would hold. He reassembled the clutch using washers pirated from our different bikes as spacers. It worked! I will again point out that I was not one of the clever and adaptive ones. Once someone on Mike's arcade asked how many baffles I had on my muffler, I was stumped. After endlessly responding to such questions with, "God, I don't know." I tried bluffing only to learn that my answers were consistently ludicrous. Finally, I said to hell with pretending to be conversant on motorcycles and became more relaxed by admitting my mechanical inadequacy right up front.

The only way to assure yourself a room at Mike's is to get there before it sells out. Sleeping on the pool table or the floor was the alternative. Occupancy is maximized by cramming as many beds into a room as the room will accept. You don't complain, for amazingly, it has its own bath and protects you reasonably well from the elements. However, men snore. Tired men snore a lot. Tired men with a half dozen cervezas and lot of Señor Paco shooters in them can rack up the decibel charts. Pillows are thrown, men shaken and "shut the fuck up" yells punctuate the nights. Then the ranch dogs would start, howling at imaginary beasts and generating midnight responses from the clients of the inn. What a cacophony of sound! On many winter nights we slept in our bike gear, as the blankets were thin, the air cold and the oil burning portable heaters subject to breakdown. When working, these heaters are effective and belch huge waves of heat into the room. They also throw off enough fumes, that if you want to by-pass a Mexican funeral, you leave the window open.

Checkout is always a great surprise at Mike's. The room rate seems to change at Mike's whim, and there often was an extra meal either included or ignored. The bar bill is on the Mexican honor system; their honor. The bill is always paid in cash dollars (no American Express vs. Visa rivalry here), and you always leave scratching your head. The experience of Mike's is priceless. You depart on an emotional high; you have just experienced a unique part of a special place, and you ride away sitting just a little bit higher and straighter in your seat as you recognize that you really must be one of the chosen ones.

THE THREE SISTERS

Earlier I mentioned successfully traversing the then infamous Three Sisters (a feat in itself especially on your rookie trip). I say "then infamous" for a by-pass to the Sisters was built a number of years ago and the old route has fallen into disrepair. What's a little disrepair if its genesis was an engineering debacle? I speak of the Sisters in the present tense, as in my memory the Sisters still remain dramatically alive today.

Below Puertocitos, the Sea of Cortez coastline turns from flat to steep and rocky. Over a period of 8-10 miles, are a series of particularly difficult grades, the Three Sisters, which tower above the sea. These bluffs drop to the sea so abruptly that, in most cases, the road was built up the walls of the canyons on the Sisters' slightly less precipitous backsides. Being distant from the wisps of coolness blown from the sea, these canyons can be hotter than the sands of Hades.

The grades themselves probably have less than a 300-foot rise in elevation but they cling to the wall of the chasm leaving larger and larger drop-offs as they increase in elevation. Wrecks of old cars plaster the bottom of the canyon and several crosses noting fatalities can be seen wedged into crevasses on the roadside. The only soil on any of the grades was provided by a mysterious and gnarled old man who could occasionally be seen with wheelbarrow and shovel, filling in some of the worst gaps between the rocks. It is difficult to imagine where he might have come from and harder to visualize whom if anyone might employ him, but if he was in an area where we could stop, we always left this "Custodian of the Sisters" a few dollars.

A number of years ago Buck Jones and I rode the Sisters together. We both are fair complexioned and it was a very hot day. We were riding Hondas, which are notorious for their obstinacy to restart once killed in the heat. To further complicate things, we were overdressed, for on a very hot day, we had made a questionable decision to pursue protection vs. comfort. As I mentioned, the road was rocky. The uphills were especially difficult because many of the rocks on the roadbed were boulders, and there was no established path through them. We had to power the machines over ledges that were up to three feet high, and while it may look easy when they do it in motocross, even better than average riders struggle with them. If not, why were the Three Sisters so notorious among all the Baja riders?

We invariably would kill the engine and periodically drop the bikes on those ledges. We would then have to jockey several hundred pounds of inert steel to a place that was level enough to have a go at starting it again. We had to kick-start these bikes, an effort in itself on a cool day, and it was as if the Hondas had their own mind and were saying "up yours, you can work for it if you can't take better care of us on these grades." We would kick over the engine 10-20 times (with only a couple of the kicks being promising), rest a few minutes and get back to kicking. Finally, for some unknown reason, Senor Honda relented and the bike would start. By this time, Buck's face had become the color of an old Soviet flag, a precise reflection of mine. We prayed that we would get on up and over the grade this time and sometimes we did, only to be felled by the next Sister. More endless kicks, longer rests and now we could feel the heat prostration coming on. We would curse the fucking Hondas, but it helped not a whit. The canyons had hit at least 110° and we had run through all of our water. Then we would try again. The kicking, by this time, was accompanied by numbing fatigue. Then on the last Sister, Mr. Wonderful arrived, Dan Sweet. He had ridden back down the grade to help. With Buck and I on the verge of heat prostration (verge hell, we were there), Dan with skill and endless energy lashed at the recalcitrant starter pedals, fired up the bikes and one at a time rode them to the top. Buck and I dragged our sorry asses to the top to be met by two running motorcycles and Dan with a huge grin. All that was left was the descent to the flat beach below, Nachos Camp.

Nachos Camp was a dot on the map (Baja maps seem to note anything where a human may have resided at one time) but it was only a pair of waterless vacation homes that we had never seen occupied situated on a lonely stretch of sand beach. God, with such a beautiful location why no people? We weren't surprised to find the houses were empty again. Even with the Sisters behind us, Buck and I were into heat stroke and any salt our bodies may have contained was now caking our skin. We stripped and immediately waded into the sea, absolutely the most appreciated dip we had ever had. Our body temperature began dropping and we started to feel better, but our system was still void of water and we *had* to have something to drink. Our other companions, who had fared better than us over the Sisters, gave us the little water they had left but it wasn't enough. It was thirty miles to Gonzaga Bay, and we didn't know if we had the strength to ride through more tough terrain.

Just then, one of the little miracles of life occurred. As we lay in the shadows of the beach houses, trying to regain some strength, a water truck appeared down the sand wash from the base of the mountains. He was hauling water south to Gonzaga Bay. None of us had ever seen a water truck on this road (or for that matter, any back road of Baja) before, but there he was. Do you think we asked for agua purificada? Not on your life! We gulped some of the best tasting water on the face of the planet from an open tap on the truck, relishing every rejuvenating drop. The crisis had passed.

PETER MARR

THE SNOWSTORM

It was November; usually a great riding month for Baja, as the air was cool and the clouds short on rain. We had a big group, which is always difficult to control. About eight of us including a newer and younger friend, Randy Berg along with Bill Ostrom, Bill Inglis and his son-in-law, Don Heser, had trailered our bikes to Mexico, crossing the border at Tecate. Tecate is the best of the border towns. Is "best of the border towns" an oxymoron? It was much smaller, cleaner and lower keyed than Tijuana or Mexicali. We drove ten or fifteen miles east where we parked the vehicles at the Pemex station near the base of the coastal range. We also had a Toyota 4x4 driven by Dan Sweet, who was not riding. Dan hated driving behind anyone (in theory, driving a "sag wagon" requires taking up the rear) and Forrest, his friend riding "shotgun" was new to Baja so their value, other than carrying our gear might have been considered dubious. Most of us were experienced Baja riders, however, we had only done the minimum preparation required for a dry autumn mountain ride.

We enjoyed chamber of commerce weather on the ride south to Mike's although one of our riders mangled a tire near the lumber camp a couple of hours into the trip. He left the motorcycle with Ramona, the trusted *bodega* owner and continued in the 4x4, as we were running late. We knew the November days were short and we knew we could fix the tire on the return trip.

Mike's was clear and crisp. The following morning, when we headed north for home, big cumuli had filled the sky, and the rain began before we reached the Valley of Trinidad. As a result, rather than riding the backroads, we shifted to the parallel highway, Mexico Numero 3, the paved road running from the Sea of Cortez to Ensenada. We gassed up in Ojos Negros, a small characterless grid-like town on a large high country plain. From there, a fairly good graded decomposed granite road went north another 40-50 miles terminating on the busy Tijuana-Mexicali highway a short distance from our cars.

While dirt, this road was quite scenic, lacked any steep grades and could be easily navigated by a passenger car. It had a couple of picturesque streams crossing it, a number of groves of old leathery leafed California roble oaks, a placid blue mountain lake and several small forests of pine. It was devoid of population other than three or four ranchos including one spread in the highest valley of the route that could have been used in a John Wayne western. It was a nice run, but what we had never recognized in all of our prior rides, was just how much altitude one gained when climbing to the rather subtle pass (you really didn't know you were going over the high spot) beyond the last high rancho. It was at least 5000 feet in elevation and incongruous as it may seem for Baja, it could get snow.

But before starting on this road, we had to make a detour, the half hour up the hill to the east of Ojos Negros and the lumber camp where we had left the incapacitated bike on our way south. By then it was early afternoon but we took longer than we anticipated fixing the tire and it wasn't until late afternoon that the bike was repaired. It was here that we made our first of several mistakes. With snowflakes falling at the lumber camp, half of the group left camp and proceeded down the hill to Ojos Negros. The days were short, the light was vanishing and they wanted to get an early start, as riding at night in Mexico (especially when only a few of us had headlights) is to be avoided. Randy and I finished up and headed down the hill a few minutes behind Dan and Forest, the driver and shotgun of the 4x4. The snowfall was increasing by the minute. We were relieved when we lost altitude and the snow turned to rain. Shortly after we took our turnoff to the north, we again began to climb and the rain again turned to snow.

Another mistake: I was the more experienced rider and knew the area well, but I put Randy in the lead as we headed north into the dark, on a slope so gradual that the only way we really knew we were climbing was the increasing snowfall and a lowering visibility. It was a wet snow, and we shivered as it breached our lightweight clothing and turned our gloves into frigid sponges. We would reach down, place our gloves on the hot

PETER MARR

manifold of our engines and glance at the steam rising from them wishing our bodies could be so warm. As we climbed, the snowfall intensified and deepened until it had reached about six inches in depth. Occasionally we could see the tracks of those ahead of us until the new snow covered them, but we neither saw nor heard any other signs of their existence. It was just Randy and me. The road was still passable and I had ridden it many times before but it was real squirrelly, and any more snow would bring us big trouble. On any surface, two wheels are much less stable than four.

Now in the dark, I approached the highest valley and could make out a ranch house by its flickering lights glimmering a half mile away across the snow-covered meadow. The road led away from the rancho and trying to approach the house across untracked snow simply wasn't feasible, but that wasn't my problem. My real concern was that Randy was gone, out of sight! I had lost him. I chattered to myself under my icy breath, "Goddamn him, he knows better. He is responsible to watch the guy behind him". But no Randy. I was alone and very cold and starting to get very scared.

The road followed a fence line and I remembered from past rides that there was a shallow ditch between the road and the fence. It couldn't be seen now as it was buried in the snowdrifts. However, the fence line was a godsend since there was now 6 to 8 inches of snow on the ground, and the road itself was indistinguishable from the terrain. At least there was a fence to follow. My bike floundered through the snow leaving a serpentine trail, and then wham! I lost it, veered towards the fence and softly sank upside down into a drift filling the shallow roadside ditch. I was pinned under the bike. I was unhurt but knew that the white stuff I was in was in reality, deep shit. It took several minutes and a lot of my remaining energy to extricate myself from under the bike and out of the ditch, but the bike was not budging. Damn, I had to get it out of the ditch and upright so I could restart it and get the hell out of there. For ten or fifteen minutes I labored, panting like a racehorse at the eight furlong mark, trying to find the strength to get the bike out of this silly little ditch and praying that Randy would have noticed my absence and return to help, but no Randy!

BAJA AND MOTORCYCLES

Just as I was close to becoming desperate, I saw a dim set of headlights way back on the road from where I'd come. I became mesmerized by its approaching glare. Several minutes later, a four-wheel drive Ford Bronco appeared, and two surfer types in slaps, Quick Silver T-shirts and shorts jumped from its cab into the snow. The 4x4's woofer was booming "Mamas and Papas" tunes into the Mexican highlands. Virtually barefoot, they waded into the snow and the three of us got the bike upright and running. They were taking this road as a short cut from San Felipe back to San Diego and that was my good fortune. They said, "Follow our tracks", and disappeared as suddenly as they had arrived, with strands of "California Dreamin" lingering in their wake.

Now I had several miles of a truly beautiful groove to follow over the last little pass and down the switchbacks to an arroyo where I finally could leave the snow behind for good. Some distance ahead I came upon the group. A couple of the guys were having a worse go of it than I was. Bill Inglis's son-in-law, Don, had broken his leg, and Bill Ostrom had frostbite and looked awful. Randy was there as well, waiting for me and once I removed my helmet, I unloaded on him. He was unperturbed and obviously, to give the devil his due, wasn't aware of the "buddy system".

The group was huddled at the side of the road trying their best to keep dry in the rain. Dan, with Forrest in the trail vehicle, had not taken his typical position as front-runner but had become disoriented and wandered back tracks in the snowy mountains before finally locating the riders. They needed to get Bill and the injured Don into the vehicle and retrieve Randy's car and trailer so that he could pick up the remaining bikes and riders who couldn't fit in the Bronco.

Randy and I rode on to the Pemex station to pick up his car and trailer. I went into a shivering fit for almost an hour before the Mexican family who owned the station stripped my wet clothes and put me in front of their potbelly stove. Randy took 45 minutes to get warm and then drove his 4x4 and trailer back to the dark and desolate roadside where the others were waiting in discomfort and wondering where the hell the help was.

I have often relived the ending of that ride with some shame and remorse. I was ashamed that I lacked the strength, in spite of my violent shivers, to quickly get in the vehicle and return to help the others on the roadside. At the very least, I could have shown some leadership so that the "roadsiders" got some help in a hurry. To this day, Dan and Bill have not forgiven Randy for, as they see it, looking to his own warmth before seeing to the miseries of others who were stranded on an empty and desolate rainy Mexican road. They may have been too harsh on someone more contemplative and deliberate than they, and if any fingers are to be pointed, they could be pointed in my direction just as easily.

As it turned out, this was my last off-road ride. It's ending had left a sour spot on my palate for a few months, and before I got over it, I had a climbing accident in New Zealand which ended my off road career. All things pass in time. The sour note is long gone, and you have probably observed that it is a sport and a venue that, even with its risks, discomfort and stress, has left a terribly positive and indelible impression on me. The people were special, the sights unbeatable and the chance to get to know the Baja from its depths to its edges unforgettable. So, I shall forget about the few negatives, and let the good times roll.

IRELAND
I'LL HAVE A GUINNESS

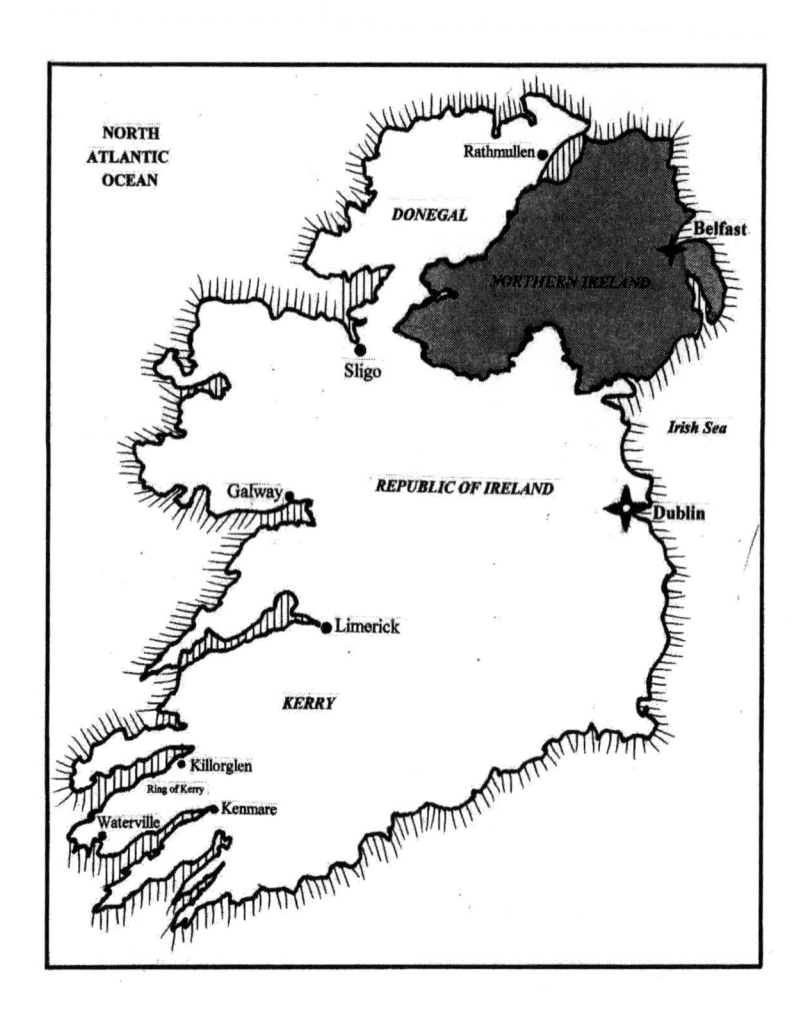

"I loved the spirit of the people and the ubiquitous emerald green of this beautiful isle"

IRELAND

I'LL HAVE A GUINNESS

Now you don't have to enjoy a drink to enjoy Ireland, but it is a real-leg up if you do. I first visited Ireland in 1953 while still a teenager and the joys and shortcomings of alcoholic libation had yet to settle in on me. I loved the spirit of the people and the ubiquitous emerald green of this beautiful isle. Where else in the world does roadside vegetation of mottled red and green banks of fuchsias grow so fast it has to be sheared with giant combine power cutters? While over the years my fondness for spirits has increased, my fondness for the spirit of Ireland has grown at even a faster pace.

So many inconsistencies exist in this wonderful little country:

- ☐ Road construction workers wear coats and ties.
- ☐ Small town police stations in North Ireland hide behind wire screens to prevent the IRA from lobbing bombs into their precinct rooms.
- ☐ A zither player practices his art at the top of a remote, windy and mournful mountain pass with his soft hat at his feet poised for a donation. Should an offering be forthcoming, out comes his CD album for sale.

- ☐ The thatched roof cottage is on the verge of extinction. The thatching art has waned. The populace has become too successful to want the hassle needed to acquire this skill or spend the time to master it.
- ☐ The country has gentrified. It is now a "have" nation and has lost the "have-not" status that cursed it for centuries. With an extremely literate populace, Ireland has become the darling of the high tech multi-nationals as well as a bright star in the arts.
- ☐ A small town near Galway is overwhelmed by crowds bringing their crippled loved ones to be cured at a notable church. Juxtaposed is the nearby pub where the foxhunters are congregating before the chase.

KENMARE

Perhaps my favorite small town in Ireland is Kenmare on the southwest coast of County Kerry. It is a nice mix of farming community, trading center and scenic tourist attraction. None of the three seem to outstrip the others. It sits at the farthest most reach of Kenmare Bay that separates two of the country's most dramatic peninsulas, Beara and Iveragh with the latter being circled by the most splendid and scenic road of Ireland, the Ring of Kerry. Kenmare is a compact town with paralleling main streets where you can find a market catering to locals next door to a woolen goods store attracting the tourist trade. At the top of its main street cresting a woodsy knoll jutting into the tidal bay is the Park Kenmare Hotel, which seems to have been transformed into a park with its formal gardens and forested islets.

The hotel is special. While it is not the most luxurious hotel in Ireland (although it is certainly in the Top 10), it is very civilized in an Irish way, which means it doesn't take itself too seriously. The bar is elegantly paneled in oak, serves about any Irish whisky yet conceived and always seems to have a barman with a special gift of gab—certainly a bartender with a gift of gab is a national treasure. Shirl and I appeared before dinner one night and were seated in the beautifully decorated lounge where we first ordered a drink and then our dinner before being seated in the dining room. From a piano in the corner of the bar room, we could hear a pleasant combination of pop and show tunes. On closer inspection we saw the piano player was a priest; a priest who happened to be an exceptional piano player. We later learned that he recently reached retirement and was from the Dublin diocese. His proclivity to alcohol was causing problems in his home parish and, in essence, his bishop exiled him to an old friend, the hotel manager at the Park Kenmare. He played the piano for his keep. It was a practical solution that worked for everyone: so typically Irish.

The dining room serves gourmet food and is quite a bit fancier than the typical Irish eating-house. As I remember, it had the only Michelin star in the country for a while. Shirl and I were eating alone and keeping our voices down so as to fit in with the tenor of this rather formal room. While enjoying our appetizer, she looked across the room and said, "My God, but I am sure that is Terri Martin". Terri is an old friend of hers from the states whom she had not seen for some time. Shirl is spontaneous and she immediately walked across this elegant room to see her friend. As Shirl faced her, Terri, in a three-digit decibel level laden with surprise, burst out with "OH SHIT, IT'S SHIRLEY!" The immediate reaction of the dining room was deadly silence. Then the ice was broken. A giggle, followed by an outright guffaw led to an utter breakdown of decorum as the whole room joined in. Dinner had already become much less formal.

Just down the street, Paddy's Pub is a little more relaxed and a whole lot more plebian than the hotel. Al Scheu, Clark Booth and I had been golfing, and making an early morning tee time at the windswept Waterville course meant leaving town at the crack of dawn. As we left Kenmare in the early morning light, we saw the entire main street being lined with low temporary fencing to accommodate the flocks of sheep that had been brought from the countryside for the monthly sheep sale. When we returned from golf in the mid-afternoon, some of the sheep were still in place but by this time, many of the herders were falling down drunk. We decided to have a pint at Paddy's, the most boisterous spot on the street. The premises were unadorned and rowdy. We were the only non-herders in the place and very sanely kept a low profile.

There was one woman inside, a crone of both indeterminable age and tooth count with her head resting on a rickety table an inch deep in stale beer. A similar layer of ale covered the floor. The sheepmen at the bar were poking each other, laughing riotously and bragging of the prices they had received for their ewes, when the door swung open. In stumbled a scruffy herder struggling to carry a huge ram with horns as long as a century and a pair of gonads the size of saddlebags. Apparently he had just acquired the animal and was bringing him into the pub for its first Guinness. Somehow they managed to pry open the poor beast's throat and pour down a half pint of stout. At this, the ram decided he had had enough of Paddy's and bolted for the door. On his way out, he knocked over several chairs, one table and one small Irishman. We quickly followed.

IGGY

Shirl and I were having a pre-dinner drink at a small hotel near Rathmullen on the Donegal coast. The hotel's pub was in the cellar. The Irish seem to have a proclivity for taking windowless space, turning it into a pub and naming it "The Dungeon", "Flanagan's Gaol" or some such similar description. The pub was virtually empty, and our only company was the bar keep and two Irishmen quite serious about their Guinness. Shirley broke the ice as only an attractive out-going woman can, and soon we were in deep conversation with the men. The more gregarious of the two offered that, "My name is Ignatius Malone but just call me Iggy." Iggy had a definite spark to him and was a walking encyclopedia on Ireland. He could talk of Irish migrants to America, Irish literature, Irish jokes and all other things Irish. Iggy wanted to know if we had Irish ancestors. I answered that I had two great-grandmothers from Ireland, one from County Cork and the other from County Sligo. "And what would be their names?" he asked. "Annie Waters and Annie Moran", I said, "but I don't know which one comes from which county." "Well," replied Iggy. "I come from

PETER MARR

Sligo and the Waters family is indeed a very well-known family there. They must be your kin." He noted that there was a pub just north of town called "Waters" that was owned and operated by a Johnny Bedford who had married a Waters. Iggy told us that Johnny Bedford would never take less than three minutes to pour a Guinness, scraping the foam from its head five or six times in the process. When finished, he would add a small shamrock of foam on its top. Iggy insisted we stop in and observe this feat when we passed through Sligo.

On a rainy morning, two days later, we drove into Sligo from the north and saw the name "Waters" on a bold sign in that wonderful Gaelic font that is perpetuated by Irish shopkeepers in every town. It was a rather grim day, and both Shirl and I looked at each other as if to say, "Do we really want to be in an Irish pub at 10:30 in the morning?" We decided of course, that the opportunity was too good to pass up.

The pub was small: no bigger than a living room in the states. The southerly half was occupied by a seedy little convenience store featuring last week's veggies. The opposite side of the room had 4-6 tables and a fine looking bar with a half dozen bar stools all occupied at this hour of the morning. As we walked in the front door, conversation at the bar ceased and all heads turned towards us. This was definitely a local hangout, and we certainly weren't locals. We walked up to the bar and I asked the bartender if Johnny Bedford was in. He replied, a tiny bit harshly, "and who'll be asking?" "Peter and Shirley Marr", I said, and quickly added, "friends of Iggy Malone. Iggy tells us that you're the finest bartender in Ireland and would never take less than three minutes to pour a Guinness!" He responded with a big grin and stated, "Any friend of Iggy Malone's is a friend of mine. I'll pour you a Guinness." Iggy was right, Waters did carve us a shamrock and took over three minutes scraping and pouring before serving. Neither of us knew enough about our ancestors to know if we were related, but after the less than warm welcome, Johnny Bedford certainly treated us as if we were long lost cousins.

Before leaving Iggy back in Rathmullen, he had asked where our next destination was. We told him we were headed to Galway for the Oyster Festival. "The city is totally booked for the Festival," he said. "Would you be having a hotel room?" We didn't. He informed us that he had a room that he wouldn't be using and it was ours if we wanted it. We took his offer with a grain of salt, for after all, he was an Irishman who had been drinking and who had such of a gift of gab that we knew he had kissed the Blarney Stone more than once. A couple of days later when we arrived in Galway and rather timorously told the room clerk that we were to have the room of Ignatius Malone, we expected the worse. To our surprise, Iggy had called, the skids had been greased and the best room in the house was ours. Oh, we of so little faith!

The Festival was a hoot. One night we were asked to join a bachelor's party that was hitting most of the pubs in downtown Galway. Fortunately the groom-to-be soon passed out before we did saving us from facing total inebriation for having kept up with a veritable drinking machine. On our second evening, the hotel had a band concert featuring the All Irish Band from Belfast in North Ireland. They proved that while the north and the south of Ireland have major political differences, the people get along famously. We spent several hours partying with the band backstage in between their gigs. How many places in the world accept strangers with the rapidity and generosity that the Irish do?

Iggy was a total stranger met for just a few hours yet he went out of his way to see that we received an insider's view of both his country and his countrymen. I would love to tip a Guinness with him some time and say, "Thanks Ignatius. You're what Ireland is all about."

MOTHER'S MILK

The west of Ireland is my favorite part of the country. Not unlike the American west, Ireland's west is harsher, less populated and the people possibly more independent than those in the greener softer east. Most of all, the west is a land of contrast. One day you are picking up an old man hitchhiking on the lonely Healy Pass on the Beara peninsula. He turns out to be so drunk and so incoherent that you never learn how the blood caking his face and arms got there. In counterpoint, the next day you are stopping at a seafront restaurant in Waterville and listening to a gale volume wind howling outside while the surf crashes over the breakwater. This was done in front of a roaring fire, eating smoked salmon and listening to Chopin in the background. How civilized can it get?

Or it may be you are playing golf on some of the world's finest links courses such as Ballybunnion, Lahinch or Waterville. They all border the sea, are treeless, windy and tough. You walk if you want to play and unless it is the dead of winter, you'd better obtain a tee time well in advance. The caddies range from schoolboys to crusty old veterans with a flask in their back pocket to ward off the wind and the rain. Inclement weather seems to be part of the mystique of Irish golf. Incidentally, Patrick, our caddy in Waterville carried double and always worked for Tiger Woods and Payne Stewart when they arrived early to practice for the British Open. At Waterville, they could practice in isolation, "far from the madding crowd." Patrick could read a putt as well as the pros. Kevin, my caddy at Ballybunnion, was still in grammar school. He had no idea of the break of the green, but he had the eyes of a hawk. He could find a ball wherever it was hit. Believe me, I sorely tested him.

On this particular golfing trek, I was joined by Al Scheu and Clark Booth, who earlier had survived the ram at the pub in Kenmare. We had booked into a small and quasi-remote lodge on Lake Caragh off the Ring of Kerry. After registering, we were informed by the manager that they were shutting down for winter on the following day and their dining room would be closed that night. They had planned a party for the staff at Nick's in Killorglin, the closest town to them, and they asked us to join them. Now Nick's turned out to be somewhat classier than Paddy's back in Kenmare. This was no pub; it was a dinner house. Here in the "outback of west Ireland" was a crowd of yuppies that would have made Santa Monica envious. When I had first visited Ireland, this area was thatched cottages and dirt-poor potato farmers. Now it was up-scale. Perhaps Ireland has had its renaissance; it has become a leader in the computer age and delightfully finds itself the fastest growing economy in Europe. Nick's still was very Irish and perhaps not as domesticated as it appeared. Clark and Al had been drinking Smithwicks Ale since arriving in the country and thought that they liked it. The bartender at Nick's felt that he had to set them right. Rather derisively he suggested that they switch; "Smithwicks is weasel piss," he muttered. "You should be drinking Guinness; 'tis mother's milk!" They actually switched and became fans of Guinness, a vile, heavy black ale that is delicious only in Ireland.

THE BIG MAN

Mark FitzGerald is a big man. He is big in stature and very big in personality. He lives in Ballsbridge, a choice, in-close neighborhood within Dublin. His office is on Merrion Row, a picturesque square in downtown Dublin. Mark had established Sherry FitzGerald, one of the premier Irish real estate property companies. Sherry FitzGerald had offices all around Ireland. Mark was interested in joining the international network that had in part, been established by CB Commercial, my firm. Tad Jones and Derek Butler, both close friends and business associates, were with me in Dublin to see if Sherry FitzGerald might be a good addition to our network. Mark and his commercial president, Killian O'Higgins (absolutely one of the finest Irish names I have ever heard—and a fine man in addition) were anxious to join this network and had worked out a grueling and impressive agenda for our 36-hour visit. It included a helicopter view of Dublin, meetings with key Irish business people, a real estate tour of the city and a dinner with Mark's partners at one of Dublin's finest private clubs.

Mark met our flight from London at the Dublin Airport and we drove into the city through the streets of North Dublin, one of the less savory districts of the capital. We were waiting for a traffic signal when two young thugs ran from an adjacent alley, broke the front window of the car in front of us, reached in and grabbed the purse from the woman driver and disappeared down the alley before we could even react. Mark showed his true mettle here as he called the Irish equivalent of "911" then rushed to the woman's car where he consoled the badly shaken woman for 15 minutes. She had been carrying £2000 in cash from the family's restaurant. Every indication was that it was an inside job.

Mark was aghast, and I know he had to feel that fate had conspired to put Dublin in its poorest light. I don't think the status of our deal ever entered his mind, just that his guests had been exposed to a part of Ireland that need not be shared. He didn't have to be concerned as Derek, who was from London, and Tad and I, with our Los Angeles roots had plenty of exposure to some very unsavory characters.

The piece de resistance of our visit was a dinner that evening with all of the Sherry FitzGerald partners and their wives. It was held at a wonderful old private club that, on the face of it, appeared every bit as stuffy as London's best clubs on the Pall Mall. The food and service were exceptional however the occasion called for endless toasts that led to substantial hooting and hollering, behavior totally unacceptable in those fine London clubs. To top it off, Tad, using his best Irish dialect, began regaling the group with Irish jokes. Perhaps it was a bit risky to tell Irish jokes to the Irish, but Tad's brogue was excellent, the jokes funny and the locals raucously appreciative.

Dublin does not shut down early and when we emerged from our last pub at 3:00A.M., foot traffic was still heavy and platoons of busses were still busy taking celebrants home after a night of reveling. On our way to the hotel, our driver dropped Mark off at his home in Ballsbridge. Mark's father, a former Premier of Ireland, lived with Mark and his family, which meant that a guard hut, complete with security man had been placed in Mark's front yard. Mark walked by the hut to say good night to the guard. He did not disturb him; he was asleep! Only in Ireland!

KOREA

301st COMM. RECON
Uijangbu, Korea

"Lines of houses were built right down to the road, and mothers would hold their little tots with snot incrusted upper lips over the dirt roadway where they would relieve themselves as the convoys would pass"

KOREA

FROZEN CHOSEN

Those of Korean heritage have prospered in America and it is quite obvious to me why! They prefer to operate a subsistence convenience store in the worst "war zone" of South Central L.A., work 18 hours a day and 7 days a week in their own Koreatown restaurant or sew straps on an endless line of bras than return to Korea.

Admittedly, I am prejudiced against Korea. I was there as an enlisted man in the U.S. Army for four months in the winter of 1955-56. The Korean War lasted from 1950 to 1953 (although at times it appears to be still ongoing) and brought great devastation to a peninsula that lacked much appeal to begin with.

Just think. The TV classic M.A.S.H., depicting an American medical unit in the Korean War, was filmed in the most unattractive portions of Southern California, and they still look better than Korea. Korea is a place that seems to have no redeeming features. Since my time in Korea, I have experienced over 100 different countries, none of which have bumped "Frozen Chosen" from the top of my list of undesirable locations. But then, I have never visited Afghanistan! Still, for total lack of appeal,

KOREA

"Frozen Chosen" as we called it, holds a special undesirable place in my heart.

Now, by the time of my arrival in Korea, duty there wasn't that bad. The war was over, drinks were cheap in the Enlisted Men's Clubs and even privates had houseboys. I was assigned to an Army Security Agency unit out in the boondocks between Seoul and the DMZ (De-Militarized Zone), the heavily armed and patrolled border between North and South Korea. Our closest civilization was Uijongbu (pronounced Wee'-Jong-Boo), an ugly little town, now an ugly big town I am told, where the headquarters of I Corps were located. I Corps had a very identifiable patch we all wore on our shoulders, a black center circled by white. The troops endearingly referred to it as "the skunk's asshole". It was appropriate to the geography. To make matters worse, I don't think the general who ran I Corps had too much clout. On Christmas, I Corps got Cardinal Spellman while Yung Dung Po got Bob Hope and a cast full of leggy blondes. We did, however, acquire some local talent at our small base. The Kim Sisters (who after an appearances on the Ed Sullivan Show gained some stateside notoriety) had plenty of notoriety among the GIs. A deuce and a half (2 ½ ton truck) took the Kim girls back to Seoul after they visited our compound for a singing performance. Some GI's bargained for spots on the trucks, as reportedly, the travelers received some unimaginably rustic sexual favors. These favors were produced on a very rough road in a poorly suspended canvas topped truck with the temperature 20 below zero outside and maybe 20 above inside! The returnees had some great tales upon their reappearance while the rest of us had to return to our dog-eared *Playboys* for gratification.

Uijongbu was a dusty accumulation of dwellings on the main military highway north from Seoul. Lines of houses were built right down to the road, and mothers would hold their little tots, with snot encrusted upper lips over the dirt roadway where they would relieve themselves as the convoys passed by. Some three miles north of town you turned west on a narrow dirt road, passed a M.A.S.H. compound and dead-ended at the 330th ComRecon situated on a creek across from a tiny village. The village was so insignificant that, if it had a name, we didn't know it.

The mission of the 330th was not dissimilar to that of the America's NSA surveillance plane forced down over Hainan Island in 2001—intercept and interpret Chinese military communications. In a highly secured fenced compound within an even larger secured compound we worked around the clock monitoring frequencies where we suspected we would find Chinese military radio traffic. In the Korean War, the Chinese had initiated a technique of verbalizing Morse code intermixed with Mandarin in their transmissions. The Americans were losing something in the translation. To combat this, some of us who had been trained in Morse code were sent to further schooling in Mandarin where we had learned to count to 10, understand some Chinese radio palaver and say a few cuss words. Listening to the Chinese "live", only made us realize how woefully inadequate we would always be in the language. Fortunately in Korea we worked with DAC's (Department of the Army Civilians) who, in this case, were native Taiwanese Chinese and they were able to supplement our meager linguistic capabilities.

It was dull, tedious work and only "spooks" in echelons much higher than ours could speak for its value. Perhaps a clue as to the merit of our operation was that after four months, the Chinese Voice Morse Intercept unit was shut down, the DAC's returned to Taiwan and blessedly, our mission transferred to the garden-like Kyushu in southern Japan.

Our Korean shifts were tiresome. Occasionally, after your third pot of coffee, you might discover a clear signal that was on the air long enough to call in the DF's in the field. These were roving Direction Finding trucks that would get a fix on the signal, and by triangulating their reading with that of another similar DF truck in a separate location, could pinpoint the location of the Chinese sender. While we hardly thought of ourselves as an indispensable cog in America's security apparatus, finding a strong enough signal that could be tracked became our own little personal accomplishment. We never did learn the results of any our work. Our data was sent on to TA (Traffic Anaylsis) and CA (Cryptographic Analysis)

KOREA

and from there, presumably disappeared into the huge database of the National Security Agency.

The 330th was pretty much at the end of the line but it did have Quonset huts rather than tents. When I originally reported for duty and was ushered to my bunk by the houseboy, the only other GI in the hut was sitting on the footlocker at the base of his bunk. On closer inspection this turned out to be more than I had bargained for, as I could see that he was soaking his unit in a glass bottle filled with a vile looking purple liquid. Overcoming my shock, I asked just what the hell he was doing. He explained that the purple stuff was what M.A.S.H. had given him to cure his penis of the chankers or chancroids, an ulcerated venereal disease. For such reasons, most GIs swore off sexual relations in Korea, gutting it out for the more sexually sanitary Japan when they rotated there every six months on R&R.

Cigarettes were the currency of post war Korea as invariably they have become after all modern wars. Each GI was entitled to buy one carton a week, and the smokes were used to pay your houseboy or buy sex (if you weren't allergic to that purple fluid), two of the very few things you could buy in Korea. The nameless town on the creek supplied sex but as with most areas more than 50 feet off a main road in Korea, it was off-limits to off-duty GIs and it was reasonably well patrolled by the Military Police. However, to confuse the MPs, the whores constructed *"koojie holes"*, and when raided, the GI would exit the hooker's abode through one of these holes cut into the dirt floor. He would drop down the mouth of the hole and angle out through a tunnel exiting this outlet through the bank of the creek. From there he would race across the frozen rice paddies back to the guarded 330th, which, because of its security mission, was off-limits to the MPs. The MPs hadn't just fallen off the *kimchi* truck! They knew of the *koojie* holes, so would usually leave one of their own outside the 330th gate when making a raid.

One night a corporal from our outfit made a rapid retreat down a koojie hole when the MPs started knocking on cathouse doors. It was February, and he took the straight line across the frozen paddies while the MPs stayed on the slower route following the levees above them. Throughout Asia at that time, human excrement was collected nightly and used for fertilizer. It grew the damndest oversized carrots and turnips you have ever seen, but eating them would give a Westerner a major sized case of the trots. Well, it had to be stored someplace, and in the corner of one of the paddies was a "shit-pit", which due to the warmth it generated, did not freeze. The hapless corporal hit this at full speed, broke through the thin veneer of ice and plunged into six feet of night soil. The M.P.'s just left him there. A night in the stockade was much more lenient than being in shit up to your neck in a *koojie* hole. While he weathered this experience, it was an example of a second good reason to wait until Japan for one's sexual endeavors.

Dogs have to be one of the major casualties in any Asian conflict. In Korea, the camp dogs disappeared with monotonous regularity usually to appear as the much-desired "extra" ingredient in a stew pot of *kimchi*, an utterly horrid batch of fermented cabbage and other delectable items, that left one with a case of halitosis that would have even knocked out the Turks. The houseboys had a nasty habit of selling our camp dogs to the villagers for *kimchi* garnish. One clever little dog named Ediwah, which means "come here" in Korean, seemed to lead a charmed life, as he must have escaped a half a dozen times to return to the more friendly compound of the 330th ComRecon. Life remains constant however. Viet Nam veterans will tell you that the locals constantly looted their units, and the thieves' most prized acquisitions were camp dogs.

The Korean War was a United Nations action and while the Americans bore the majority of the responsibility (as well as the casualties), many other nations were involved as well. While the Kiwis and Ethiopians had great reputations as fighters, perhaps the Turks were the most renowned in that area. They were so ferocious and tough that the Koreans were scarred shit-less of them. An interesting dichotomy later arose as friends who served in Viet Nam told me that the South Korean soldiers there were considered the most vicious and frightening of any of the national armies involved in the conflict. The Viet Cong would totally bypass a Korean position rather than face them. Everything is relative I guess.

One glacial day, several of us were invited to visit the Turkish Regiment for lunch. It was bitterly cold, and with the wind-chill factor maxing out, we could have been peaking Everest with Hillary and Norgay. As we entered the Turks' camp we had to ford a stream that was at least a foot and a half deep. Parked in the middle of the stream was a deuce and a half truck with two Turkish privates, barefoot with pants rolled up, washing it. I still shiver thinking about them.

We had heard that the Turks sliced off the ears of their vanquished enemy as trophies. We didn't quite believe this, but above the desk of the Officer of the Day was a large photograph with two grinning Turks holding six feet of clothesline between them—strung with human ears. Guess it was true!

We told the Turks that back at our unit we had great problems with the *"koojie boys"* (I guess everything a GI came into contact with in Korea was a koojie-something or other) who would come over, under or through the compound fences and steal anything not bolted down, even up to the size of generators. This was in spite of having armed guards walking the fences all night. The Turks found this amusing and said they had never experienced such things at their unit. Small wonder!

As a nation, South Korea has made a tremendous comeback since their Civil War that turned into an international action. It has prospered due to the persistence of its people and their hard work. I admire them for bringing themselves from a third-world nation to first world status in less than a half a century. Korea is not a place I desire to see again. I grant you I was there during a difficult time and an unfriendly winter season. Seoul is now a large and sophisticated city and has hosted the Summer Olympics and the World's Cup. It can't be anything like it was. I sometimes use it as an example of what I don't like, and all of us need visions such as that. Perhaps it is best that my memories of it are not disturbed.

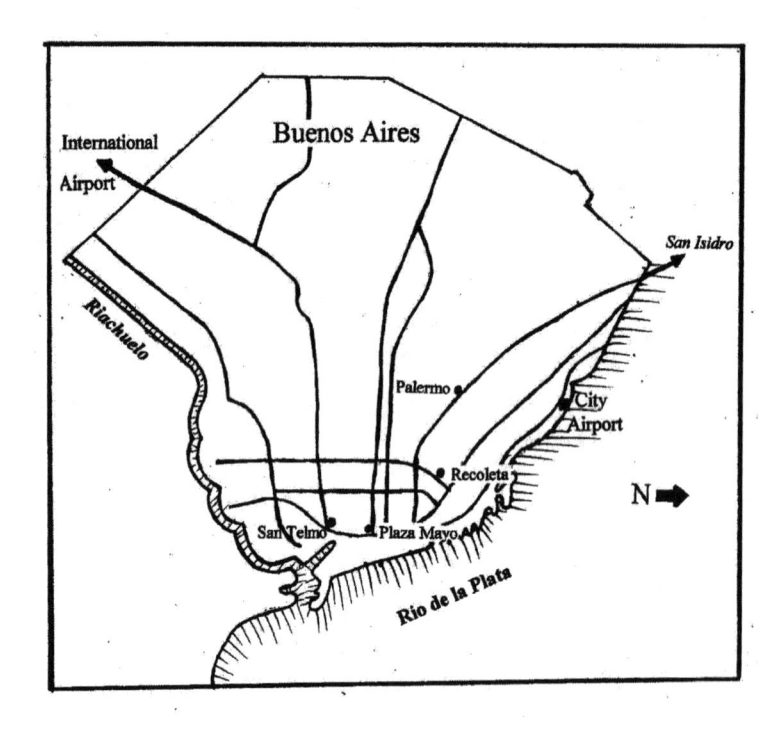

BUENOS AIRES

" Some great looking lothario who bore a definite resemblance to Al Pacino in "A Scent of a Woman" was instructing Shirl in the finer points of the tango and I began to think that maybe this wasn't such a great idea after all"

BUENOS AIRES

A PLACE TO TANGO

Buenos Aires is a very special city. I love it. This is certainly not due to the natural beauty of its location, for it sits on a vast plain fronting the Rio Plata, an unattractive muddy slate colored river. Actually the Plata is tidal and looks an awful lot like a bay to me. It measures over 50 miles across to Uruguay on the opposite side. That's a river? For pure physical impact, Buenos Aires could be Omaha, Nebraska.

Buenos Aires is the eleventh largest city in the world, and Argentina boasts the highest standard of living in Latin America. While its financial stability has been subject to wild fluctuations, it still qualifies as a "have nation", and as such, the Argentines rely on imported labor to do the difficult work. In the U.S., the Mexicans usually do the tough and menial work. The Filipinos bear this duty in Southeast Asia and the Turks in Germany. In Argentina it is the Andean cultures that do the work that locals spurn. These people are usually Bolivian or Peruvian and the faces you see manning the trash trucks, washing dishes or walking the beams on high-rise construction sites are mostly Indian.

It is the people and to a large degree, their culture that makes Buenos

BUENOS AIRES

Aires a special place. Both are very European. The envious Brazilians to the north like to say that the Argentines are nothing but elitists. They speak Spanish, have Italian surnames and wish they were British. In a candid moment, most Argentines would confirm this. Unlike almost any other country in South America, their ancestry is primarily European. The Buenos Aireans are often referred to as Porteños, which derives from *puerto* or port, indicating, "they just got off the boat".

The British and the Argentines have had an interesting historical relationship. Springing from a European heritage, the Argentines looked toward Europe more than the U.S. Their relationship with their forefathers, the Spanish, was preordained. Early on, the British, an international trading powerhouse, and the Argentines began a long love-hate relationship. The British-Argentine confrontation over the Falklands (be sure to call them the Malvinas when in Buenos Aires) was somewhat startling because the two countries seemed to be so civilized. But territorial prerogatives have overwhelmed civility before, and the Falklands became just another example. It was a short ugly little conflict, and at the time, an Argentine professor was quoted as saying, "the war was like two bald men fighting over a comb."

Buenos Aires is a city of *barrios* or neighborhoods, and much of the city's population live their entire lives in the same barrio and relate to the *barrio* more than the city as a whole. On the afternoons when the soccer teams (River Plate or Boca are two of the most notable) play, their working class *barrios* come to a standstill—perhaps save the saloons. On the other end of the economic spectrum, the close-in Recoleta district is like the East Side in Manhattan; sophisticated, elegant and leafy with expensive high-rises mixed with elegant old homes. This is where you are apt to find most of the fine hotels and many of the more chic restaurants. Incidentally, Argentine dinners start late. It follows its Spanish heritage and custom calls for dinner to begin about ten. Only famished Americans are finished by that hour.

The Jockey Club, across from the French Embassy, represents the highly sophisticated center of social life in Buenos Aires and particularly within the Recoleta *barrio*. They take their pedigree seriously for at their suburban club they not only have two golf courses, but a racetrack. I had thought the R.A.C. (Britain's privately owned and very prestigious Royal Auto Club) in London with its dual facilities on the Pall Mall and the Surrey countryside was the ultimate, but the Porteños may have gone one up on them.

The Jewish quarter is adjacent to the Recoleta, very self-contained, with some of the streets having the flavor of the rag districts in New York or Los Angeles. The Jews are a major influence in Buenos Aires where they control the clothing business and are a huge factor in real estate, finance and other related businesses. While the Jews have been extremely successful in Latin America, I have been told that only Mexico City has as influential a Jewish community as does Buenos Aires.

The central business district is a shopping cornucopia. Narrow side streets punctuated by wide boulevards make you think you are in Paris. Shopping complexes, which would be the envy of Manhattan or Knightsbridge, are inserted onto cramped sites to take full advantage of the heavy foot traffic. The Galerías Pacifico is the most noteworthy of these centers. It is a multi-storied atrium mall in the heart of the city, an attraction supposedly patterned after Milan's famous shopping gallery, Vittorio Emanuele. Buenos Aires' principal shopping areas are fringed by office hi-rises along the river, while the old adjoining dock area, Puerto Madera, has been renovated with cafes, small offices and specialty shops.

Palermo, Recoleta's residential neighbor to the north, while also studded with high-rise apartments, displays more openness taking advantage of their spacious parks. Many of the embassies have located in Palermo. Palermo is the closest choice neighborhood of single-family homes from the downtown. Palermo is Buenos Aires equivalent of Hancock Park in Los Angeles, Pacific Heights in San Francisco or St. John's Wood in London.

Wide landscaped boulevards with up to six or eight lanes in each direction connect these neighborhoods with those to the north. Forget the lanes, the Argentines do! In my first trip to Buenos Aires in 1993, my friend Luis Ramos, the proud owner of a very responsive BMW, drove me up one of those boulevards to his home in San Ysidro, 20 hair-raising miles to the north. It is a beautiful suburb, and Luis has a spectacular wife and family. That drive, however, shortened my life by an Argentine summer, and I hate to think what it's doing to Luis!

On one visit, Luis hosted a professionally cooked *asado*, or barbecue, for our group. A vegan would have slit his throat. Salchicha, a spicy sausage, as well as lamb, pork and every part of the carcasses of a small herd of beef cattle were offered. I am not a big meat eater, but we had some guests there that were. What was left over could still have fed the entire Argentine army for the duration of the Falklands War. As you might recall, it was quite a short war, and to be truthful, the army not very large.

Luis is a most remarkable man. He runs a very successful commercial real estate company in Buenos Aires and was light years ahead of his competition in recognizing the impact the computer would have on his business. His English was minimal, but as soon as he saw he was on the threshold of having an alliance with a major U.S. company, he took an English cram course. Two months later, the CB Alliance had its first meeting where all of our Latin American partners were drawn together in Coral Gables. Luis gave his 15-minute part of the program in English!

THE CATENAS

We met Nicholas and Elena Catena at Los Lingues, an historical working ranch and resort ninety minutes south of Santiago, Chile. Los Lingues has been in the same family for 16 generations. It has been accepted as a member of the prestigious Relais and Chateaux group. My wife, Shirl, and Elena immediately became fast friends and during our stay, rode horses, talked, hiked, talked some more and explored this most dramatic locale at the base of the Andes.

Across the Andes from Los Lingues is Mendoza, Argentina's Napa Valley. The Catenas farmed wine grapes there and owned Latin America's largest winery. Nicolas told me he produced 11 million units, second in the world only to the Gallo Brothers. I, too concerned that I might look stupid, never asked him to clarify if that was in bottles or in cases and if it covered a year or a month. That leaves plenty of room for interpretation and dismisses any in-depth knowledge I might have felt I had about wines. In any case, it is a lot of wine.

In addition to running the winery, Nicolas is an economist and received his PhD from M.I.T. where he later taught. He held an informal financial post with the Argentine government, and I suspect were he still there, at least some of their economic crises could have been averted. Nicolas is a quiet almost shy, unassuming man. His wife, Elena is somewhat younger than he, quite attractive and very outgoing. She initiated a startup computer company and has a most probing inquisitive nature. Above all, she has a love and a flair for that most graceful of dances, the tango. In Buenos Aires, the tango is more important than commerce and almost as important as fútbol.

Buenos Aires has any number of tango clubs and theatres. The Alvear Palace Hotel in the Recoleta has a Las Vegas-style show, beautifully staged and performed. To this observer, two hours of watching formal tango begins to drag and frankly, the men are too good looking and the routines too conventional. This showy type of tango was definitely not Elena's style, and one night after dinner at their home in Palermo, Elena announced that we were all going to a tango club in San Telmo, the Greenwich Village of Buenos Aires. Nicolas begged off immediately, but a young houseguest, Vicente, was commandeered to be her escort, and the four of us headed for San Telmo.

San Telmo is near the river, a series of narrow streets laid out in the typical Buenos Aires grid pattern. Funky stores, lots of antique shops and small bodegas pepper the barrio. The tango club had a modest exterior, and upon entering, we discovered the inside was no grander than the outside. The room was long and rectangular with seats on three sides and a small bar and a jukebox along the other wall. No band, no frills, no ambience. Apparently this club was for serious dancers.

The tango is a complicated, stylized dance, and the male does all of the leading. As neither Vicente nor I had a clue how to dance the tango, we were destined to be spectators. Lovely Elena knew however, and Shirl, while having absolutely no idea how to tango, is after all attractive and dauntless, so the two of them would have no trouble getting partners. Vicente and I were given instructions to follow them into the club by several minutes, sit on the sidelines, and give no clue that we had ever seen them before. That would assure them lots of offers to dance.

Elena, decked out in a leather skirt, was asked to dance immediately. She looked fantastic and danced the same way. One great looking lothario who bore a definite resemblance to Al Pacino in "A Scent of a Woman" was instructing Shirl in the finer points of the tango. I began to think that maybe this wasn't such a great idea after all. Shirl struggled for a few minutes learning the moves, but being a quick learner and having a series of men more than willing to teach her, she soon looked like she belonged there.

Meanwhile, Vicente and I sat on the sidelines trying to look interested while drinking pitcher after pitcher of beer and going along with the sham that we had never seen these women before. The girls had nothing to worry about. They were attractive women, incognito in a nightspot and escorted by a pair of invisible men who couldn't dance. We did, however, qualify as a "fail safe" should the women decide they needed an escape hatch if they were "wantonly" solicited.

The club was obviously a spot for serious tango aficionados and even though the jukebox must have played the music from "Last Tango in Paris" a half a dozen times, the X-rated behavior that the ubiquitous Brando brought to that film was not repeated. Almost two hours after our nearly mutual arrival, a sodden rag doll jumped into my lap. It was Shirl. She was exhausted. She looked like she had just finished her second circuit of a Boston Marathon that had been held in a sauna. Her odyssey finished for the moment, she was returning to the ennui of her American roots.

The experience said something about this city that perhaps is missing in the U.S. We were not slumming. This club was a meeting spot for people from different economic status and backgrounds to share something they love: the tango. No expectations of anything more, no hustling, just a common interest. Would you find this gentility, this sensitivity in Greenwich Village or Newport Beach, California? I think not.

EASTERN EUROPE

EMERCO, the acronym for the Europe Middle East Regional Courier office, was one of three worldwide offices established by the U.S. State Department to move diplomatic mail to its embassies.

EASTERN EUROPE

COVERT AND BYZANTINE

EMERCO, the acronym for the Europe Middle East Regional Courier Office, was one of three worldwide offices established by the U.S. State Department to move the diplomatic mail to and from its embassies. It was based in Frankfurt, Germany and during my tenure there in the early sixties, it housed about 40 couriers who covered the embassies and consulates in Europe, the Middle East and Africa. The mailbag-appearing pouches were moved on 15 pre-established routes (usually leaving weekly) that could entail a trip as short as two days or as long as four weeks.

Couriers usually traveled first class, not due to the largesse of the State Department, but rather because of the additional extra baggage allowance afforded first class passengers by the airlines. As it was not unusual to be escorting several hundred pounds of mail, first class turned out to be cheaper than paying the excess baggage fees on a multitude of pouches. While in theory diplomatic mail is classified, it could include such diverse items as personal mail, heavy code machines or even, in one case, Jackie

EASTERN EUROPE

Kennedy's jewels when she accompanied her husband to Vienna for a summit meeting with Khrushchev.

Getting a courier job was not easy. The requirements were: male, single, a college graduate, a veteran, at least 25 years of age and able to pass stringent physical and security hurdles. In addition, the applicant had to type 35 words a minute. The couriers considered the typing a "wash-out factor," for as the actual hiring process was in the hands of the State Department's personnel group, the Courier Service never got a chance to see the new hires until they reported for duty. Should the courier headquarters office not like the "cut of your jib" when you reported to Washington, you were asked to take a typing test to verify your prowess. The relic of a typewriter used for the test was in such poor shape that an experienced executive secretary could have failed the test. While I wasn't asked to take the typing test, courier headquarters must have had some pause after seeing me. Not only was I the youngest courier in the service, but I looked younger than I was. This youthful appearance might have been a blessing to me later, but it was not advantageous to me at age 25 when I would still get "carded" buying cigarettes! The Courier Service must have really swallowed hard as they had to supply this baby face with a GS-15 card that wielded enough power to bump a Brigadier General from a military flight. Disappointingly, I was never able to put this privilege to test.

My job was based at the American Consulate General in Frankfurt, Germany. Frankfurt, not being a capital city, had a consulate rather than an Embassy although it dwarfed most of the U.S. embassies elsewhere. By the innocuous nameplates next to locked doors in the Consulate's halls, I suspected that the Frankfurt Consulate housed many more "spooks" than worker bees. A courier job didn't pay much money for the annual salary was only $5000 per year. However, all of your expenses were covered for the 25 days a month that you were on the road, and government housing, medical expenses and PX privileges were all covered by the government. Couriers were hardly welfare cases. We were housed in very comfortable field grade military housing on Hansa Allee in a pleasant

PETER MARR

Frankfurt neighborhood. American military types surrounded us, good people, but it did tend to isolate us from many of the benefits found in the German culture. To this day, I am somewhat unappreciative of things Teutonic, perhaps influenced by the bland mixture of American and German influences, which the highly business-oriented psyche of Frankfurt had spawned. Maybe my attitude would have been different had my first exposure to the German people and society been more intimate.

THE FIRST TRIP

Shortly after my arrival in Frankfurt, I was assigned to my first courier trip. Their first time out, an experienced courier always escorted the new guys. This usually dictated an Iron Curtain trip for your maiden voyage, as two couriers were always paired on travel behind the Curtain. My first partner was Vinny Cella, a friendly, pinch-faced, little guy from Philly. He verged on being hyper but was always entertaining and knew all the angles of the job. I'm sure when he returned home, he could outtalk the best of the Philadelphia lawyers.

Tannhausen, who was to become my favorite of the consulate drivers, gathered us from our apartments two hours before flight time. He first took us to the Consulate Pouch Room to pick up and sign for our pouches, then drove the short distance to the airport. Often when arriving with large pouch loads at Frankfurt Main Airport, we looked like tour guides (minus the little national flag they generally hold up) while we led several porters bearing our sacks to check-in. Usually, we would be taken to a waiting room and a few minutes before passenger boarding, we were shuttled out to the awaiting plane on the tarmac. Vinny knew all the angles, so he saw to it that we were ensconced on the Swissair Martinliner that presumably was to take us to Zurich for the night. We were seated while the other passengers filed in and the flight attendant requested we fasten our seat belts, make ourselves comfortable and enjoy our flight to Milan! Whoops, did she say Milan? Vinny shot up like he had been hit in his midsection by a taser gun. We were on the wrong plane! Fortunately

EASTERN EUROPE

we made the Zurich flight and while it might not have been our fault (the shuttle driver had gone to the wrong plane), it would have been interesting explaining our missed flight to the senior courier officer. Bottom line, our perpetual instructions were quite basic: don't lose a pouch; don't miss a flight! It was not exactly an auspicious start!

After overnighting in Zurich, we headed for Prague; one of Europe's hottest destination spots today. However, under its communist regime in 1960, it was morosely bleak with an almost medieval feeling. It was so beautiful, so fascinating, so gray, so depressing. Traffic was sparse and primarily evidenced by Russian Ladas and Czech Skodas. Restaurants, in most cases, were run by the state and featured unimaginative food and worse service. The hotels were seedy. Make no mistake; the city was still drop dead beautiful. Prague sits in hill country, filling a serpentine valley bisected by the Vltava River, and thankfully, allied bombers had left its castles, squares, churches and bridges intact from the ravages of World War II.

We had a free day in Prague, and I guess Vinny felt I would be corrupted by all of this beauty and decided we should go to the Prague Stadium to see the Spartakiada, a Russianesque display of hundreds of young people waving flags and banners and slithering along the stadium floor. The pageantry was endless and so boring that we returned to our hotel on Wenceslas Square, sat at a small table on the sidewalk, drank an indescribable aperitif and watched the Skodas go by. I have returned to Prague several times since its liberation from communism, and the changes have rendered this version of it almost unrecognizable. The good news is—there are new restaurants, fine hotels, stylish shops, a feeling of prosperity and legions of upbeat people. The bad news is—there are people, lots of them.

Our other destination on this short trip was Warsaw, a city that was a far cry from Prague. First of all, its location on the Polish plains does not have nearly as much oomph as Prague. Prague's rival in Poland is Krakow, three hours by train southwest of Warsaw. Krakow boasts many similarities to Prague but on a smaller and perhaps more manageable scale. Warsaw, however, was virtually destroyed during the war, and while the city did a beautiful job of recreating its old town brick by brick, the rest of the city is a strange juxtaposition. A few stylish buildings that survived the war still remain, augmented by Russian "wedding cake style" high rises and even a few glass curtain-wall office monstrosities which, at the time of their construction, were sorrowfully considered western architectural treasures

We left our pouches at the American Embassy, situated on a tree-lined boulevard at the edge of the downtown. The embassy was to be demolished the following month and a new facility rebuilt on the site. Eventually, a combination of European bureaucracy, covert attempts by the Poles to bug the facility and an American contractor trying to work in Poland extended its construction period to seven years! The Admin Officer wanted to show us the temporary embassy then being prepared for occupancy. It was in a handsome building on a picturesque square, part of the Stare Miasto (the Old Town), an area that had been painstakingly rebuilt. The temporary embassy building was teeming with American security officers flown in from Western Europe and the states. They showed us two orange crates filled with listening devices the size of golf balls that they had chipped out of the two-foot thick walls. The security men had also discovered a conduit, two inches in diameter, coming from the adjoining building. I never did learn what the Russians and the Poles had in mind for that cable and it may have been a decoy. Our security staff obviously felt that they had missed some of the bugs, as over a year later, the only spot in the embassy where classified material could be discussed was inside the safe!

Recently I returned to Warsaw to find a much more interesting city. The Polish economy has been the best in Eastern Europe and has also seen the largest influx of western capital. It had a bounce and a pride lacking from many of its "fellow travelers" in the Warsaw Block. I had returned to Warsaw as an old Arizona pal, Daryl Lippincott, had asked me to speak to the membership of CEREAN, a group of Eastern European private real estate companies. Daryl was a director of a group that had received a grant from the State Department to encourage private enterprise in Eastern Europe through the build-up of its residential real estate industry. Under communism this type of enterprise didn't exist, and Daryl's group had done much towards establishing a backbone that filled a major need. My speech was translated into five languages, the results of which seemed to elicit different responses from different ethnic groups. One reaction didn't vary in Magyar, Russian, Polish, Slovak or Czech however. My attempts at humor fell flatter than a skillet full of Russian blintzes.

THE AARLBERG ORIENT EXPRESS

One of the more memorable courier trips was Route 108. It traversed Hungary, Rumania and Bulgaria and, as the airline schedules were spotty and especially difficult during the winter months, we often used the train. We would catch the Aarlberg Orient Express in Vienna, have a trainside pouch exchange in Budapest and continue east to the express's termination in Bucharest. Now this train was a far cry from the famous luxury train, the Orient Express, which was the setting for Agatha Christie's *Murder on the Orient-Express* and Cruella de Ville's method of escape to Paris in *101 Dalmatians*. Today, the Orient Express can pamper you from London to Venice on a 24-hour trek for about $2000 per person. The Aarlberg Orient Express consisted of several battered wagons-lit cars but lacked all amenities most notably a dining car and a club car. It did, however, have compartments with berths. Even if on schedule, the train took upwards of 36 hours for a trip of less than 600 miles, so we had to take provisions to eat while aboard. With Eastern European train stations offering modest culinary potential, we took bread, cheese, canned goods and lots of sterno for our minuscule portable stove. For entertainment, we carried a small short-wave radio that accessed lots of martial music. At times, Willis Conover's cool jazz show on the Voice of America, the highlight of the VOA schedule, would come through.

The train followed the Danube eastward between the two spectacular cities of Vienna and Budapest. It then crossed the plains of central Hungary before entering Romania. After Arad, it climbed into the scenic, but somber and brooding Transylvania Alps, countryside hauntingly recounted by Bram Stoker in *Dracula*. The train left the mountains at Ploesti, whose oil refineries were bombed by American B-24's in 1943, and continued across the plains to Bucharest where we usually had a two night layover (unless we were taking an overnight roundtrip to Sofia in Romania) before repeating the trip in reverse.

Prior to World War II, Bucharest had been known as the Paris of the Balkans, but by 1960, after 15 years of Communist rule, it had fallen quite a bit short of its former glory. Like Paris, it did have wide boulevards and monuments, but no Seine, no Eiffel Tower and most of all, no ambience. Fellow courier Carl Caruso and I hit town the week between Christmas and New Years and were invited to a party by the Embassy's Admin Officer, Bill McGovern. Bill picked us up at our hotel that evening and explained that we had another stop so we could pick up his girlfriend Pamela, who worked for the Canadian Embassy. Several blocks after leaving the hotel, he commented almost as an aside, "Oh this is interesting. You are being followed tonight. I have my regular tail but we have a second one as well." Apparently couriers weren't considered much of a threat to the communists, and it was rare that we were followed. But as we pulled off the wide boulevard into the narrow side streets to pick up Pamela, it quickly became apparent that we had a budding entourage. After we left her home for the party, a third car, Pamela's regular tail, had joined the caravan. Bill said; "Let's have some fun!" He sped up and started turning sharply down side streets and up alleys as the tails careened behind us, not unlike a scene from Mack Sennett's "Keystone Kops". After a few blocks, Bill pulled over to the side of the road and let them all catch up. He waved at them and they waved back with big smiles on their faces. Bill explained that he didn't want to piss them off and it made no sense to "cry uncle" as he really might need to ditch them sometime in the future. The party that night was a little anticlimatical.

The best "Iron Curtain courier story" I have heard was an incident that happened prior to my time as a courier. The Orient Express usually had

EASTERN EUROPE

one of its wagons-lit cars (sleeping cars on European trains) filled with couriers from several countries. In addition to our American pair, you might find a British Queen's Messenger, a twosome of French, a Japanese and even on occasion, a Russian. We seldom socialized with the others (save the British QMs) for the French acted aloof, the Japanese kept to themselves and the Russians were the enemy. Thus, we usually just hunkered down in our compartment. Now the Italians didn't have a professional courier service at that time, but still had classified mail to transport. They would ask for volunteers from their Foreign Office in Rome who might want to take a leisurely trip on the Orient-Express, spend a couple of days in Bucharest, and return to Rome. They had plenty of takers who must have pictured the Aarlberg Orient-Express in the same grand manner that I had.

One summer in the late fifties, the Italians were returning to Rome after their layover in Bucharest. Since the ride was a long one and they obviously had to travel in comfort, their first step was to change to their silk pajamas and lounging robes. This particular train was loaded with East German girls returning to Berlin after taking their vacations at seaside resorts on the Black Sea. What a field day for the Italian couriers. As the train loaded, they stood in the aisles in their pajamas, murmuring "bella bella signorina" and practicing the old Italian art of "bottom pinching" on any young woman moseying within their range. Ultimately a pair of young ladies suitable to the Italians tarried. They were immediately asked inside the Italians' compartment for a Cinzano or a Kir Royale, the ingredients for which were predictably on hand. Typically, the Italians were carrying Cassis and Gorgonzola and the Americans canned Vienna sausages and Snickers bars!

It wasn't long before the German girls succumbed to Italian brio, but they had a complaint. The Italian couriers' compartment was filled with pouches and the canvas sacks were hardly conducive to any type of a bipartite téte á téte. The Italians quickly solved this problem by calling the porter. They had him lock their pouch-filled compartment, and then they escorted the girls to their compartments in the adjoining car. There they spent what was presumably a rapturous night.

The Italians were to learn they had a number of problems.

- ☐ Problem number one: Couriers never leave their pouches unattended.
- ☐ Problem number two: They were with a pair of ladies in a Communist country behind the Iron Curtain in the midst of the Cold War.
- ☐ Problem number three: During their sojourn, the train had reached the railroad yards in Budapest. So, two hours earlier, the Italians' car was disconnected, hooked to another train and departed for Vienna. Unfortunately, the girls' car was heading for Berlin in another hour!
- ☐ Problem number four: They were in their pajamas and not in possession of any of their clothing, passports or pouches.

So, there were two Italian couriers in the Budapest Bahnhof, without money or passports, dressed in their pajamas with their pouches soon to be in the possession of an unfriendly foreign power. Not a stellar performance. The end result was that they screwed up a mighty fine deal for all the young chargers in Rome's Foreign Office as shortly thereafter, the Italian government initiated their own full time courier service.

Moscow

Of all places, Moscow always held a unique, almost arcane mystique for me. It was just so alien, not so much exotic as foreign. When I am reminded of Moscow, the adjectives that come to mind are dark, dreary and brooding, unlike say my vision of Paris where I have a sense of brightness and life. If requested, my inner mind is able to conjure up a gloomy day in Paris and a sparkling day in Moscow but only with sustained effort.

Today, with upwards of five million Americans qualifying as millionaires, it is hard to relate to the $13.00 per day that the U.S. Government approved as per diem in 1960. This amount was supposed to have covered our hotel, meals and incidental expenses. Believe it or not, in Russia we made money on this per diem. First of all, Moscow was very inexpensive. Secondly, the ruble was a soft currency, and the USSR prohibited moving it in or out of their country. Obviously, this greatly reduced its value outside the USSR. As couriers carried diplomatic passports, we were not subject to search and almost always came into Moscow with rubles. These were rubles we had purchased at the Deutsche Bank in Frankfurt at 50 to the dollar when the official rate was 10 rubles to the dollar. We rationalized this "indiscretion" on the basis that it only hurt the Russians, and after all, they were our enemies! It was just a little scam, and we took pains not to "rub it in" with the Moscow Embassy staff. They were under way too much scrutiny to pull off such an action even had it been readily available to them. Inside the USSR, you were limited as to what you could buy (samovars and babushkas only went so far), but we still returned with major amounts of caviar. With our manipulated exchange rate, our cost for a two-ounce tin of beluga was less than a dollar. The caviar and vodka parties back at our Frankfurt base were legendary!

When Washington wanted to communicate with Moscow, it wasn't as simple as today. Radio and facsimile communications did exist but weren't always available and were subject to intercept. Most of the classified material had to be sent by diplomatic pouch. The pouch went through a rather convoluted journey to get to Moscow. First, some kind of classified document was pouched at the State Department in D.C. and escorted across the Potomac to the military's pouch room at the Pentagon. From there it would be escorted to Andrews Air Force Base where it would be turned over to a military courier or, on occasion, an off-duty military officer on a hop. Basically, a hop was nothing more than a member of the military hitching a ride. This escort would take a military flight to either Paris-Orly or Rhine Main Air Force Base at Frankfurt where he would leave the pouches at permanent pouch rooms maintained at those two airports. The daisy chain continued when a Frankfurt based State Department courier would dash off to Helsinki, our gateway to Moscow. He was usually met at the Helsinki airport by two more American couriers temporarily assigned to the Helsinki Detail who were poised to fly to Moscow via Finnair or Aeroflot. At Sheremetyevo, Moscow's principal airport, they were met by a driver who took them directly to the Amerikanski Pahzolstava (the American Embassy) where the pouches were finally dropped off at the pouch room. Only then was the Ambassador delivered his two-day-old issue of the New York Times!

The Moscow hotels were basic, and each floor featured an old woman seated at a barren desk monitoring the comings and goings of all guests. This was a good job for these poor souls as they were inside. They could have been wielding brooms on Tverskaya Boulevard sweeping the constantly falling snow into a berm of ice running down its center. Our usual hotel was the Gastinitsa Ukrainia, (Ukraine Hotel), a 30 plus story birthday cake monstrosity. As decent private restaurants (or more accurately, any restaurants) were scarce, most of our dinners were at the hotel. Chicken Kiev and shashlik were our favorites since we knew what they were. Four wines were available; Georgia #1, #2, #3 and #4. The Georgia referenced was the home state of Josef Stalin, not Scarlett O'Hara! Two of the wines were red and two were white, and they were coarse enough to push you to vodka. One of the few culinary options was the commissary at the American Embassy where you could get sandwiches and some simple western fare or down on the Moscow River at the Amerikanski Domo (the American Club) where the staff of all the western embassies hung out for films, bingo, burgers and a lively bar. At that time, it had to be Moscow's only "body exchange".

If our Moscow visits seem sheltered, they were. Should a Russian stranger approach us more than once, however innocently, we were ordered to report the incident. He or she was assumed to be a Russian agent, as the average populace was under orders not to associate with westerners. The KGB worked very hard trying to compromise anyone in the Embassy, so caution was preached. To combat this, all the western staffs were granted extra benefits that included lots of trips to the west. As a pleasurable aside, the western embassies were populated by some of the most attractive and "friendly" girls ever assigned embassy duty. I am not sure this wasn't

EASTERN EUROPE

by design, as these very appealing western girls became a very viable "thinking man's" option to some of the beautiful Russian women used by the KGB to "chum our western waters" while attempting to subvert our staffs.

I should clarify the Helsinki Detail. The couriers had an apartment in Helsinki, a pleasing if frigid city in winter, where we were detailed for six weeks. Two weekly round trips to Moscow were scheduled. The apartment in Lauttasaari, a pleasant seaside neighborhood, was a nice respite from hotel life and the Finnish women were lovely, friendly and sometimes seductive and liberal. The twice-weekly trips into Moscow were interesting. Weather was often inclement, and the planes were virtually empty in the winter months. On occasion we had to forsake the western standards of Finnair for the Russian airline, Aeroflot. Their Ilyushins and Turpolevs seemed serviceable but nothing else seemed to work. They were always late. Check-in was laborious and cabin crews must have been recruited from the Moscow Circus. I actually stood behind a pillar at Sheremetyevo watching a mechanic standing on the wing of an Ilyushin while he refueled and smoked a cigarette simultaneously!

Taking the train from Helsinki was a lazy and pleasant breather from bad weather flying and the train was scheduled every other week. The train became necessary as the U.S. government had to ship a large amount of surface pouches into Moscow. These pouches were unclassified and in the west, could have been assigned to the captain of an American carrier such as Pan Am or TWA for transport. Surface pouches usually consisted of written material that was non-time sensitive. But in the case of Moscow, they were used as the supply source for both the American Commissary and the American Club. Obviously the Americans couldn't rely on the Russians (to whom a Mad Magazine was the anti-Marx) to cooperate in the shipping of films, western music and foodstuffs for their employees. In Moscow, it was so easy to get blinis or caviar that they could actually become tiresome. A plain old American cheeseburger was much in favor, and their ingredients had to be imported through the pouch. This type of courier duty was not as glamorous as the old films with Adolph Menjou hiding behind pillars with his pouch padlocked to his wrist. If pressed, we had to admit that the job was not much more than a glorified mailman. The train took the better part of 24 hours including a stop in Leningrad. As with the Aarlberg, it lacked a dining car but large Russian peasant women were always on board serving endless portions of tea forcing you to frequently use the lavatories, a hole cut in the floor of a bitterly cold compartment at the end of the car. Life along the Russian rail lines must have been somewhat pungent in warm weather.

For an American courier in 1960, life in Moscow was certainly agreeable and interesting. We were rarely followed and had free access to most of the city. We waited in line with the thousands of the faithful for a glimpse of Lenin's tomb, wandered the open areas of the Kremlin, took the elaborate subway and browsed through GUM, the expansive Moscow emporium that was more like a bazaar than a department store. Maybe, best of all, through the embassy we were able to finagle tickets to the Bolshoi Theater, an astonishing experience for such a *nyet kulturi* as I.

The communist regime was omnipresent. The Russians had managed to bug the American eagle in the reception area of the Embassy. Presumably, we didn't have too many delicate conversations in the reception area, but who knows. Two Russian soldiers perpetually guarded the Embassy entrance, accessed through a single car archway. They could not withhold entry to us (although they appeared to have been coached to give us dirty looks when we entered), but if you were a Russian who wanted access, you had better possess a document from Khrushchev if you expected to get through the arch.

One night at the Hotel Ukraine, Frank Nesci and I were snowed in and having nothing better to do, consumed a prodigious amount of very good Russian vodka. Finally, we retired to our room where earlier we had discovered a wiretap in the bedside lamp. Believe me, it was a pretty rudimentary tap or the pair of us would never have discovered it. We cozied up to the bug where we proceeded to curse Nikita's ancestors and belittle his sex life. If the KGB translators ever got around to listening to

EASTERN EUROPE

our low level palaver, they must have assumed that this pair of doofuses were never going to be a threat.

After a 35-year absence, I returned to Moscow in the late nineties. It looked the same: more cars, some new buildings, not as clean but certainly recognizable. If you even looked American, people not only talked to you, but in fact, sought you out to practice their English. Private enterprise was rampant, and young entrepreneurial American real estate developers were making fortunes. American and Western European corporations had also discovered Moscow, and the boom brought unprecedented demand for office space. This led to huge profits that led to graft, that led to the Russian Mafia. Unfortunately, many who got in bed with the Russian Mafia experienced fatal intercourse.

On one trip, my host, Conrad Peterson, a California expatriate with a Coldwell Banker background, took us to a lap-dancing club, an experience that would have been totally contrarian in the former Communist era. Somewhat atypically in Moscow, there was no cover charge for Americans; all others were charged US$100. The dancers were gorgeous and the house collected $75 for allowing the girls the privilege of being pawed for three to five minutes. From a practical point of view, had we been interested in employing them, it would have been out of the question. Russian gangsters in attendance were completely monopolizing two or three of them at a time. For that much money, it was hardly to our chagrin. It was interesting to see the American lap dancing culture so demonstratively exported.

On two different occasions during the following year, I visited Moscow while holding possible merger conversations with a Russian/American real estate firm led by a brilliant young Alabaman, Miles Jones. Miles and his partner, Bill Lane, were fluent in Russian and had made every effort to blend into the Russian community rather than just become a part of the "Anglo-American colony", a practice followed by most American expatriates. In a short visit he gave Shirl and me great insight into how Moscow's business community operated. The wheels were just coming off the Russian economy since the ever-present graft had ultimately stalled the country's growth. A year later, Miles left the firm as the "bubble" had burst in Russia and real estate had contracted a case of "severe bleeding". Miles has stayed in Russia as a consultant, slugging it out until the market turns again.

Today, most westerners who want to do business in Eastern Europe start with Poland which is pro-business, more dependable, safer and more active than Russia. Russia's plight is sad. It truly is the sleeping giant. With an educated populace and immense natural resources, it does have awesome potential. Perhaps there is a turnaround in sight for Russia. The world will be better for it if there is.

THE NEW ORDER

By pure happenstance, Shirl and I were in Berlin on the day of the reunification of East and West Germany. We were booked on a train to Prague from the Schönefeld Station in East Berlin. Our West Berlin taxi driver, ensconced in a nice shiny Mercedes, admitted he had never been in the east and today was the first time he could do so legally and safely. He felt sure he could find the station however. We cruised across the former border at Brandenburg Gate and east on Unter den Linden, the most imposing boulevard of Berlin, a thoroughfare that had languished under the Communist rule. Now it was temporarily festooned with kiosks selling beer, wine, flags and endless souvenirs of the turnover. The hottest items were golf ball-sized pieces of the Berlin Wall. An anemic little East German Trabant, a truly awful little car, hung suspended from gigantic gallows. Its anemia, compared to the Volkswagens, Mercedes and BMW's of the west, had become the national symbol for East German ineptness.

The mood was festive, and Shirl and I were disappointed that we were missing such a good party by having to move on to Prague that night. Our driver was in the same league as a London cabbie and found the station easily. There was neither a porter nor baggage cart in sight, and having typically over packed, we had to wrestle our bags to the furthest track on an almost empty platform. As we boarded the empty car, two young men followed us up the steps crowding us from behind. Rude we thought. Upon reaching the aisle, coming from the other direction was a third man with a fourth standing in the open door of the first compartment. The fourth one dropped to his knees and began groping for Shirl's purse that hung from her wrist. Being much more intuitive than I, she yelled to me, "Peter, we're being mugged," and proceeded to knee him in the Adam's apple. He had no idea what he had taken on and audibly choked and gasped. Shirl had her man! With a hundred pounds of bags, I charged ahead like a pulling guard pretending to be a running back and knocked one of them aside. With this one-two punch, they hollered something in German and ran. Our only loss came from a pocket in the raincoat I wore. They had mistakenly stolen a tobacco pouch thinking it was a wallet.

I believe the story is relevant. Fortunately for us, these muggers were inept novices. A group of gypsies in any western capital would have picked us clean. On this first day of freedom in East Berlin, they were probably on their first job. Mugging was severely punished under communism, so they may have been anticipating a new career path. I do hope their lack of early success diverted them into a more honest career. Reality had set in. In spite of all the trouble James Bond could find in Eastern Europe, under communism, this area was relatively safe. It was not to be again.

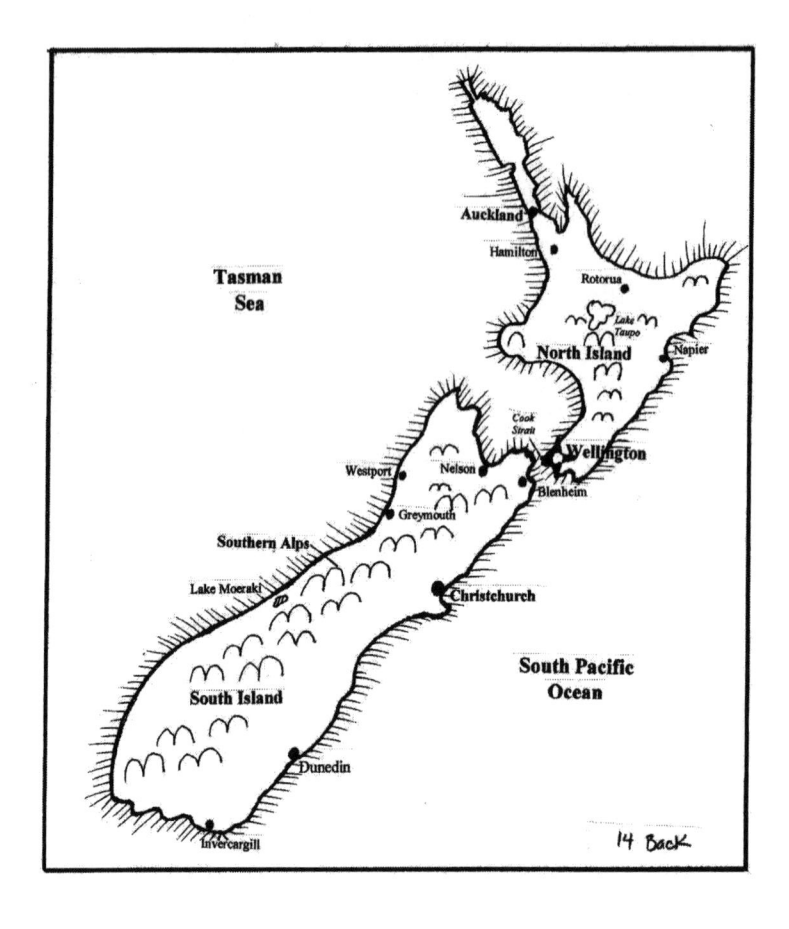

NEW ZEALAND

"We were in the middle of a two-pronged land and air rescue effort!"

NEW ZEALAND

DOWNED DOWN UNDER

February 1, 1995
South Island
New Zealand

The morning was especially crisp and bright even for a mid summer day on the rugged west coast of New Zealand's South Island. Forty-eight hours of rain had preceded this ideal "chamber of commerce" weather. This had been confirmed by Gerry McSweeney who proclaimed that his rain gauge had already accumulated five inches of moisture. Based on a lengthy overnight effort to dry our sodden clothes, we needed no reminding on this account. Gerry was our host and the owner of our aptly named accommodations, the Wilderness Lodge. Our group had reached this most idyllic of locations by bicycle the day before. Our "group" consisted of nine adults, most of whom had experienced enough living to have attended their thirty-year college reunions. In addition, there were two guides, Norman Howe and Karen Clausen, who were being very creative on extending their educational process through the joys of subsidized travel.

NEW ZEALAND

Our tour group was the temporary liege of the premier Canadian tour company, Butterfield & Robinson. B&R specialized in unique adventure filled vacations. This was the third trip that my wife Shirl and I had taken with them. On this occasion, we were trading the softness and intimacy of our trips to the French Dordogne Valley and Alsace for the brawn and wide-open seclusion of one of the world's most remote corners.

Anyone who has ever read a travel brochure or applied for a passport has heard of the beauty and isolation that are the legacies of the islands of New Zealand. The North Island has the preponderance of the population and (like Ireland) is a soft, green, undulating land a perfect backdrop for the seemingly millions of sheep. As soon as you accept these Irish similarities, volcanoes, geysers and deserts pop up to remind you that you are not in the "old sod!" Even the cities of the North Island are different. Auckland, the country's largest, has an incongruous sameness for so gorgeous a natural setting; and Wellington, the capital, looks and acts like a miniature sleepy San Francisco with its spectacular hills and harbor.

The South Island is the same size as the North, but it is less populated and even more majestic in its scenery. Its Southern Alps that run Andean-like down the west coast are snow clad, and at their feet, glaciers and rain forests coexist. Christchurch, with its 300,000 people, is the closest thing to a metropolis existent on the South Island. When you arrive in Christchurch, you swear this must be England though the globe shows the home country to be half a planet away. The River Avon does for Christchurch just what it does for its namesake at Stratford in the English Cotswolds. It serpentines through the city's expansive parks, streets and even through its central business district. The Avon smoothes its way through exquisite botanical gardens, cricket fields, restaurants, boathouses and outdoor theaters. In addition, it shares some of its frontage with the Christchurch Public Hospital, an institution I was soon to visit.

While New Zealand must be among the most physically spectacular venues on our earth, its most overwhelming resource is its people! The

Kiwis manage to come off as a delightful blend of their British/Irish heritage in some strange combination with the rough and ready antics of their closest neighbors, the Aussies. They have to be the running-est, trekking-est, playing-est lot on earth. Not only does rugby, cricket, sailing and soccer play a big part in their lives, but any game or contest worth playing will manage to sneak into their environment. This only adds to their propensity for manifesting an incredible love of life. It shows in their almost lilting "good-on-yaw-mite" which is usually said with a smile. A smile is expected in return.

Back to that almost perfect morning. We were on the fourth day of a ten-day trip via bicycle, train and van that we had originally signed up for with our friends Nancy and Floyd Brown, also from Newport Beach, California. The tour would eventually circumnavigate the South Island. Lake Moeraki, our current location, was rain forest country. Now this was not a type of rain forest filled with creepy crawlers and such. It really was ecologically sanitized. New Zealand's remote location had given it the ultimate protection from ever being the natural habitat of reptiles and other unfriendly beasts. A living ecological example is the kiwi bird, New Zealand's national emblem. Even with no natural predators, it is nearing extinction. Never having had a need to fly, it is now easy prey to the domestic pets imported by man.

The cliff-laden west coast of the South Island is a magnificent presence with glaciers, fern covered mountains and a rain forest ambiance. It combines the best of Norway, Switzerland and the Oregon Coast. It is the home of a colony of New Zealand fur seals and Fjordland crested penguins.

Gerry, our lodge proprietor, doubled as a naturalist and it was his role to guide us on a morning's walk through the Rimu and Kahikatea forest to the Whakapohai Beach in hopes of sighting the penguins. Once the beach was reached, we would follow the coast for about a mile before again turning inland to the highway that paralleled the coast 500 feet up from the water. This would leave ample time for a barbecue lunch back on the river flowing from Lake Moeraki to the sea, after which we would navigate its gentle rapids by canoe. We had been pre-warned that our trek would require "moderate fitness" and that the walk would be wet enough to need sneakers and swim gear. An idyllic adventure.

The start **was** idyllic! We tunneled into the foliage so quickly that after a dozen feet, the highway was only a vague memory. Gerry led us on a herringbone path through still-dripping fronds and greenery while making multiple stream crossings. By the time we had finished our first 100 yards, we were all soaked. Lush vegetation, small waterfalls, orchids and occasionally a vividly colored bird were our entertainment in this environment. We all said to ourselves, "It just doesn't get any better than this!" Then so suddenly, emerging from the vegetation was the coast of the Tasman Sea. The contrast was like stepping from a dark tunnel directly into an enormous Jurassic Park-like panorama. We experienced booming surf, a stiff breeze laden with salty moisture and an isolated beach creating the erroneous impression that we were the first to experience its solitude and vastness.

The beach had engaged in a losing battle to the storm that accompanied the prior day's rain. Its historic accumulation of sand, vandalized by the high surf, was waiting offshore for calm weather and gentle waves to nudge it back to its former home. Meanwhile, the shore's black rock underpinnings were exposed and walking was treacherous at best. With the combination of a rapidly incoming tide, large surf and a sandless and diminished beach, we had some suspicions that we might be in the wrong place at the wrong time. Rocky sentinels of granite jutted into the surf and while wading through the backwash of its combers, we were routinely knocked off our feet. Finally, we could go no further and Gerry, minus Norman and Nancy who, being in the lead had cleared the most difficult pinnacle, led a retreat back to safer ground. On this day, however, there was to be no waiting on the beach for the turn of the tide that would have allowed us to retrace our steps. Gerry pointed to the tree-laden escarpment at our backs and said, "Mates, put on your monkey suits. It's a stiff climb and while it will be tough, you will all make it! Besides, it is the only way out!"

Some hints of trepidation and hesitation must have been what made Shirl ask if I was OK. This climb was not really something I wanted to do, but, after all, Gerry was the expert and I've always been a great sport. Being a good sport made life an adventure at times, but the unwanted payoffs from my failed follies were lingering with me at that particular moment. While I was reflecting, Gerry had sprung to his feet and was leading the charge up the Kiwi equivalent of Gallipoli. And I followed!

The precipice we were scaling rose some 500 feet from the beach to the highway above. Its lush vegetation covered a base of shale that, combined with a multitude of roots and mud, made footing treacherous. Our sneakers were not up to the task and with an accumulation of muck on their soles, soon offered no traction at all. Gerry's route seemed to follow a faint track, but it was hard to envisage who or what might have used it before.

After a few feet, we were all steaming under a canopy of foliage. The going was to get rougher what with intricate tangles of roots, rock ledges and brush blockages that had to be traversed. Often, our fellow climbers needed assistance to get over a particular rough section. At 150 feet up the woody precipice, I reached overhead for a handhold on a very large boulder. As I pulled myself up, a man-sized portion of the boulder split off leaving me suspended for just a millisecond. Then, like a runaway freight train gaining speed, the rock and I joined for a macabre dance down the slope. We hit, bounced and flew off in diverse directions. Hit, bounced again . . . and again . . . and again. Each impact seemed to break something within me and each shock took away my breath. Even as utterly helpless as I was, my mind was working overtime. It informed me that these were quite probably my last moments alive. I felt that survival was . . . at the very least . . . uncertain. Each bounce reinforced that premonition, but I was still conscious, wasn't I? After about 80 vertical feet of bouncing, the rock and I wedged to a stop on a tiny flat shelf.

That was the good news! The bad news was that my granite antagonist had me pinned to that ledge crushing my mangled left leg. I screamed as the intensity of the pain surpassed my tolerance. The landslide I heard trailing my fall seemed of no consequence to me. The pain was overwhelming, emanating from the 300 pounds of rock that pinned me down from toe to chest, pressing my shattered shinbone, and compressing the life from me. I knew I would die if the rock were not removed immediately. It was then that I sensed activity from above and suddenly saw Gerry, bouncing down the slope with the speed and agility of a mountain goat. He reached me quickly, muttered, "hold on", and with one incredible spurt of adrenaline, lifted the boulder, sending it hurtling down the rest of the mountain into the surf below. Gerry and I skidded downward for another ten feet before sliding to a stop.

The incredible pain was instantly gone, but it had left its legacy. My vision was a deep green cloudy blur with no definition. My legs were twisted in odd ways and my entire upper body throbbed. Blood from my scalp oozed over my face. But I was alive, wasn't I? Gerry, who was himself sporting some minor bruises from our last slide, was soon joined by fellow biker Mark Schwarzman and our Butterfield guide, Karen. They had both been just above me on the snaking line climbing the grade so were now the closest to us. Those above them, including Shirl, had only heard my fall, as the forest was much too thick to visually follow my descent. Gerry hollered at them to stay where they were, so as not to risk a landslide on this most unstable muddy slope. Slowly and carefully, I was inched to as level a position as could be found in this cramped and compacted space. Gerry instructed Karen, Mark and Frederick the Finn to stay with me while he led the rest of the group up the cliff and on for help. Frederick, a lodge guest, was a humorless and dour man who had joined our group for the morning.

I could hear the rest of the group continuing up the mountain until the sound of their strenuous upward climb and muffled voices was lost in the dense vegetation. Mark made himself busy collecting water from a small rivulet that my body straddled. He would pass it on to Karen who wiped my brow and provided blessed sips of the muddy liquid. About that time, the first truly positive sign occurred. Like someone had switched on a

PETER MARR

light bulb, suddenly my eyesight, which must have faded to 10% of 20/20, came totally back. It was like an omen (actually my optic nerve was reviving after being struck) and helped provide me with a rush of optimism that I was going to survive.

Karen truly was an angel. As a guide, she may have been feeling some residual responsibility to Butterfield & Robinson at that moment, but her feelings to me flowed directly from the heart. For the next three hours she wished, loved and prayed me through the ordeal of trying to keep a badly injured man alive while waiting the arrival of the anticipated helicopter. How many times during those hours did I think I heard the early thump-thump-thump of approaching rotor blades? After each agonizing disappointment, Karen's soothing words, uttered with such obvious love and care, calmed me for the longer wait ahead.

On the other hand, Frederick the Finn turned out to be a jerk of the first order. A pampered rich man from Helsinki, he chain-smoked and bemoaned the fate that had gotten him there. After he had loudly proclaimed for the third or fourth time, that "there was no way the rescuers could get me off this mountain", I finally told him, "If this is the case, could you kindly shut up and let me die in peace." This managed to get through even his thick Baltic cranium, and henceforth, we only suffered his smoke and not his pessimistic predictions.

While we were waiting and hearing "phantom choppers," Gerry was leading the rest of the group up the cliff. He had told Shirl that I had broken my ankle, and he needed to put together a rescue party to bring me out. Shirl was so relaxed with this explanation, that she felt my injuries would merely make me an observer rather than a participant on the balance of the bicycle tour. Obviously, Gerry had managed an emotional "coup." Then he was gone; vanishing up the seemingly impassable cliff, obviously as much at home in this venue as are the Barbary apes of Gibraltar on their special rock. Shirl and Floyd Brown hopelessly looked for a spot that would bypass this cliff. Finding none, they propped their bodies into the wall by pushing their heels into granite footholds. There were justifiable tears from those that tended to be acrophobic, but their only choice was the same as was mine below. Stay put and wait for help.

My fall occurred about noon. The rescue party arrived three hours later. They came down the cliff from the highway above. In the lead was the indomitable Gerry with half a dozen other hearty volunteers organized from among the 275 inhabitants of this valley. Their numbers included a doctor, a nurse and other professional guides. Their equipment included stretchers, a chain saw and blessed morphine. First they lowered a line down the top 100 feet of cliff to allow them to rappel around the most difficult portion of the mountain. This was to be the same line used by Shirl and Floyd's stranded group to scale the balance of the precipice. With Vern Harvey, a professional guide, leading their way, they all managed to reach the top. There they experienced that tremendous exhilaration of surviving an ordeal that called for all the tenacity, confidence, patience and courage that they could muster.

Down near the base of the palisade, I was aware of the shouts of the rescue party above me, as they carefully lowered themselves and their equipment. At almost the same time, I heard that peculiar thumping noise so distinctive to helicopters. The chopper was hovering over the surf line. To no avail, they had endlessly criss-crossed the area looking for a spot large enough to put down. However its approach did signal that the incredible loneliness of the wait was virtually over. We were in the middle of a two-pronged land and air rescue effort!

The rescue team inched down the mountain shouting at each other to "be careful" and "look out for that loose spot." Down they came to me, a moving miracle constantly yelling words of encouragement about their imminent arrival. Then they were there, crowded around me on my tiny ledge busily planning this last descent to the waiting helicopter airlift. The doctor was among the first to reach me. He checked me only briefly, for in that precarious location, any serious first aid was out of the question. It seemed that the morphine injection should be almost anticlimactic with the euphoria of relief and shock I was experiencing. When the needle penetrated my arm, my cares seemed to fade away. A bright orange rescue stretcher appeared and the chain saw buzzed away creating enough space to get my ample girth moved to the stretcher. My weight at the time was 235 pounds which didn't make me easy to move. Later, doctors said my extra weight might have given me added protection from even more serious injuries. I would hate to have to make that case to *Weight Watchers,* however.

I was quickly maneuvered onto the stretcher with three men assigned to each side and one more controlling a line tied to the top end of its frame. He kept it looped around the most solid object available to him at any point in time. This was my safety belt. The plan was to take me back down the escarpment until we reached the modest clearing near the beach. From there I would be lifted into the helicopter. Slowly they wrestled me down this quicksilver slick track with the bearers awkwardly spilling over into the slimy edges of the rain forest. More than a few choice oaths hit the air for the task was not only hard work but hazardous. This team was up to the challenge, however. They got a big man down a treacherous grade that all of us had labored to scale in the first place. There were a few slips but never a fall! When we made the clearing that had been expanded by the chain saw, the chopper was hovering above the shoreline no more than 100 feet above us. The impact of its ever-reverberating engine seemed to accentuate the force of its powerful downdraft.

The rescue line was rapidly dropped from above, looped around the stretcher, and I was airborne so quickly that there was no time for even a simple good-bye or thank you to my rescuers. Wind from the blades in concert with cold air swirling off the water gave me a case of the chills as I was winched upwards. As I was raised, I was swinging like the lead ball at the end of a plumb line. Skyward, I could see the chopper with the winch man standing outside on the left strut. As I approached him, he grabbed the stretcher and dexterously manipulated its upper portion inside the cabin. Then almost immediately we rose, the strut man and my lower half remaining outside. This first ride was a short one, probably less than

NEW ZEALAND

60 seconds, and paralleled our fateful route up the escarpment. We put down on a roadside viewpoint next to a waiting ambulance. It was there that I finally saw Shirl.

She was not prepared for the sight. The only description Shirl had received on my injuries was the initial prognosis from Gerry, so all she expected was a broken ankle. Seeing me in the flesh, however, brought tears to her eyes as she surveyed my badly battered and bloody body. During this time, the paramedics were moving me into the waiting ambulance for some immediate and overdue first aid. They splinted both legs and placed a sling of sorts on my dislocated left shoulder. The shoulder socket was resting on my neck. An attempt was made to clean me up but most of the muck and blood removal was left for the hospital staff. The paramedics did move me from my relatively comfortable orange stretcher to a rock hard model less than two feet wide which would fit in the chopper. To get a stretcher and patient plus three big men into a 4-seat helicopter is an engineering feat. It was so tight that the winch man had to hold my left shoulder in place for the two and a half hour ride to Christchurch.

This trip went up the spectacular coastline to the Fox Glacier, where we refueled and on to Arthur Pass, a low point through the Southern Alps. I was told that it was a magnificent scenic trip, but all I could see was the Plexiglas canopy above me. Finally, we circled the banks of the River Avon in Christchurch and put down on the cricket fields next to the Christchurch Public Hospital.

No cricket, but New Zealand Television News along with the press and their cameras were on hand. Obviously, it didn't take much to sell a newspaper in New Zealand! An ambulance ferried me to the hospital where it seemed that half the staff had congregated to meet me. I had witnessed the TV coverage, but the incident was also getting radio and newspaper play so I was already an object of interest.

The chief of the orthopedic unit, John McKie, and his assistant, Matthew Nott, first determined the extent of my injuries and then outlined their plans in some detail. I had broken both ankles that had to be set and pinned. My left tibia was shattered with a compound fracture and an external fixator would have to be drilled into those few areas of the bone left undamaged. This fixator was a nasty looking device, which looked like a huge steel plated comb anchored in my leg with large pins. I was told that it would actually look worse than it felt, and it was used instead of a cast in serious cases like mine. My right shoulder was broken and my left shoulder dislocated. My right lung was partially collapsed, my heart bruised and my mid torso was already turning black and blue, but these internal injuries would have to wait until later—after they had put me back together again.

The subsequent surgery was the first of the five I experienced in both New Zealand and California. My medical care in both countries was top rate. The New Zealand hospital staff was badly overworked, and the hospital food was basically inedible. Those shortcomings aside, the staff was always patient, caring, efficient and long-suffering. The country has both socialized medicine and no-fault insurance, and even tourists involved in accidents receive free medical care. Socialized medicine seemed to lead to understaffing, but the hospital staff did not come up short on care. The attitude of the doctors, who under the system could not be sued for malpractice, was much more casual than what we are accustomed to in the states. After my second surgery, Matthew Nott said, "Peter, we had to put a drain in your chest today. You caught us by surprise. You must have leaked two liters of ugly black stuff all over the floor of the theater (operating room). I thought I'd hit your bloody heart." How many American doctors would feel financially secure enough to speak like that?

My most attentive Kiwi nurse was Rose Corner. She not only showered extra attention on me (even on her time off), but she constantly arranged happenings around Christchurch for Shirl. Shirl had flown in from Lake Moeraki the morning after my accident. After ten days or so, the challenge of maintaining a vigil for a patient no longer in a life-threatening situation, becomes routine. The extra time left Shirl free to explore Christchurch.

Rose took her hiking, to open air concerts in the Botanical Gardens and on family outings.

Shirl had also managed to find a room in a small cottage that came with a delightful landlady, Heather Penrose. It was central to both the hospital and town and gave her a more welcome and warm experience than she could ever have received at a hotel. On her own, Shirl was to become a Christchurch fixture during the month we were there. She was part of the scene at concerts, the theater, the opera and most of the good dining spots in this delightful city. She was third row center and backstage at the theater, a guest at receptions, interested and inquisitive about the citizens, the conventions and culture and appreciative of all the hospitality afforded her. She was a well-respected and delightful guest.

Some things from the Christchurch hospital will always stay with me. I shared a room in Ward 23, the trauma ward, with four others. One of these souls was Jimmy, a hard drinking Irishman, totally immobilized by a broken back. For the first 24 hours he was a model patient until the DT's bested him. From that point, he experienced constant and demonstrative withdrawal. He would yell and try to undo the straps holding his battered body to the bed. His demonstrations allowed me to share his sleeplessness and tabled any desires for the Bombay Sapphire Martini I might have yearned for.

There was Malcolm Ott, the Honorary American Consul, who, well beyond the call of duty, visited me four times at the hospital and guided us through the intricacies of the Accident Claims Commission that later was to pay our bills. A year or more later, I learned that the American State Department, in their infinite wisdom, did away with Malcolm's position. Finally, one afternoon there appeared an attractive stranger, a thirtyish woman who was Gerry's sister-in-law. She came to my bedside with two handsome and well-scrubbed young children both carrying bouquets of hand picked flowers. She announced that she felt that I had been in the hospital long enough to enjoy and experience the freshness of children. She was clairvoyant, and I tapped a large reservoir of tears on that one.

PETER MARR

As good as the medical care was in New Zealand, I was consumed with a yearning to get home. Originally, the doctors had strongly recommended against any early medevac, though friends and associates at home were working hard to organize one. The doctors did, however, bless a return flight after the first month of hospitalization. Immediately, Julie Owen, our faithful and tireless CB Commercial administrator at home, went to work on airline reservations. Easier said than done! Every airline was sold out between California and New Zealand for most of February and March. This was, of course, the heart of the New Zealand summer. A flight was finally arranged for February 26th, but its backup was almost two weeks later. I had to be well enough to catch that plane or suffer the endless wait for the next one. Two days before departure, I spiked a temperature of over 102°. It was the advent of a staph infection, not to be taken lightly. The night before our scheduled exodus, the staff doctors circled my bed and outlined the pros and cons for a departure the following day. Medically they thought: no, emotionally: yes. Emotion won.

Our nurse Rose and her children led a small delegation of friends to the Christchurch Airport that next day. Included were Shirl's landlady, Heather, and our friend Paul McGahan, the New Zealand tour leader par excellence. We had met Paul at Moeraki Lodge, and he had been recruited into the rescue party. This was fortuitous as his backcountry experience was unlimited. We all ensconced ourselves in the airport's Ansett Lounge while waiting for the flight from Dunedin to Auckland that would connect to the United Los Angeles flight. When the Dunedin flight was delayed and ultimately cancelled, Rose turned the lounge into a trauma center and changed dressings and administered intravenous feeding in the center of the lounge. Ansett did divert a flight and we finally did leave Christchurch, six hours late. Norman Howe, our Butterfield guide, who had stayed on the South Island for two more bicycle tours during my hospitalization, accompanied us.

Upon reaching Auckland, it was Norman with a strong assist from Shirl, who bullied our way onto an imminent Qantas flight to Los Angeles. We bought five tourist seats in the center section and were raced to the plane by the airport manager. We were the last to board. Shirl evicted two poachers from our seats and twenty minutes later, upon reaching altitude, she turned the row in economy into a bed. With her providing a continual supply of painkillers and sleeping pills, I was virtually comatose for the entire 11-hour flight to Los Angeles.

To say I have had steady progress since arriving home would be a falsehood. My recovery has been mercurial with endless interruptions. I have experienced everything from nuclear medicine to I.V. lines and was thrown the "curve ball" of e-coli and staph infections, bone transplants and massive multi-month antibiotic injections. My shattered left leg now contains more steel than Pittsburgh: 21 screws and two plates and the right leg added another half dozen screws. I have nothing but accolades for all my medical care. This, in concert with a truly wonderful outburst of loving support from family, friends and co-workers, has made my recovery inevitable and at times, even enjoyable.

Some might say I was unlucky to grab the only loose boulder on the mountain. The reverse of that is that I was extremely lucky to have been in a country that could mount an intensive rescue operation and provide top rate medical care. I dodged a lot of bullets that day and obviously, my time had not come. My Mexican partner, Arturo Sanchez, said, "Peter, if this had happened in Mexico, we would still be looking for you."

Now I have tested the danger of skiing, flying, parachuting and dirt biking over the years. Physically, I have paid a high price for those pursuits as well as for this latest escapade on the side of a New Zealand mountain. My experiences have been extensive and rewarding, my life fulfilling. I have enjoyed the benefits of broad and enriching travel, some measure of success in my career and always could depend upon a vast array of family, friends and loved ones.

All of us are charged some kind of dues as we go through life. Perhaps I paid mine February 1st, 1995, on the South Island of New Zealand.

Authors Note

This chapter was published as a pamphlet in 1995. In November of 2000, on a motorcycle trip through the South Island, I returned to the cliffs of Moeraki. From a safe and removed distance, they seemed different and not so treacherous, but this didn't lessen my feeling of foreboding. I later shared a pot of tea with Gerry McSweeney who has prospered and has opened another spectacular inn in Arthur Pass. He reminded me of things I'd forgotten. I liked him. He saved my life.

EPILOGUE

PATHS CROSSED: MEMORABLE PEOPLE

The paths I have taken through life have been multifold and have given me the opportunity to meet people of high caliber, solid character and profound interest. Some, as you might expect, were even of a contentious nature. Many have already appeared in the pages preceding this Epilogue, but those that follow have had a deep impact on my life.

Jim Didion	"I did it my way"
Bill Forbes	"Urbane but real"
Ian Mitchell	"The racist"
Shirley Schieber	"An off-the-wall lady"
Jim Stanley	"The kindly showboat"
Harvey Ranson	"A different breed"
Brian Bertha	"Energy personified"
C.Y. Leung	"The quiet mover and shaker"
Zelda Littlefield	"The Mormon influence"
Cor Van Zadelhoff	"The self made man"
Bill May	"Mr. Nice Guy"

PETER MARR

Joaquin Ayala   "The droll wit"
Bill Dobyns   "Country boy"

J IM D IDION—"I DID IT MY WAY"

Jim Didion was the Chairman of Coldwell Banker Commercial, CB Commercial and CB Richard Ellis for the better part of 15 years. This, in itself, was a major challenge with three corporate names in a single decade. Jim is brilliant and decisive and has a first class real estate mind. Of all the senior executives I have met in the commercial real estate industry, he has a better grasp and understanding of the business than any of them. In the early nineties, his toughness allowed an over-financed firm in the worst real estate market since the great depression of 1929, not only to survive, but also to emerge from this market with an expanding lead over the competition. I admire his capacity for work and his determination to be a winner.

Saying all of this, I suspect that Will Rogers never met him! If Jim sensed weakness in anybody, he was more combative than a sixth grade schoolyard bully. In a nanosecond, he could turn scathing and abusive and while I never personally saw him bring anyone to tears, he came remarkably close to getting punched out more than once. A man of major mood changes, he could be absolutely charming if called for, but seemed to enjoy his reputation for being one tough son of a bitch.

In 1985, Gary Beban and I were the two finalists for the presidency of the company. Gary, a Heisman Trophy winner at UCLA, had had a meteoric career and was extremely well liked. Because of longer tenure with the company, I was probably considered the favorite for the position. There never were any conversations between Jim and me about this opening, nor do I believe there were any with Gary. But without a doubt, the whole company knew there was a one-judge contest underway. Early one morning, Jim informed me that he had made the decision to appoint Gary president. For the balance of the morning, my ego got in the way and I was dejected. But by lunchtime, I had come to the conclusion that I was the

EPILOGUE

lucky one. Gary would have to live with Jim on a daily basis, meet his demands and transmit and justify Jim's views to a veritable army of strong and opinionated high-level managers. Jim's decisions were often unpopular, but, in any case, Gary was the messenger. Gary ended up with the toughest job in the company for which thankfully, he was well compensated. Gary became my ombudsman with Jim for which I am eternally appreciative

Jim, undoubtedly, had problems with my style. I am sure that I lacked the killer instinct that epitomizes so many corporate executives, but I felt strongly that CB's heritage called for its leadership to have a close and personal relationship with its producers. Jim's leadership style was directed outside of the company rather than internally, not necessarily the wrong direction for a chairman. The rebuttal to this is, that while your primary responsibility may be to the shareholder, unhappy employees can quickly negate shareholder profit. Had Jim chosen what might be considered "more prestigious" fields than real estate as a career, he would have been equally successful. What a Goldman Sachs man he would have been. There you were expected to make any decision (presumably assuming it was morally correct) and get it done even if you had to scatter some bodies on the way. He would have made Ariel Sharon look like a dove. Certainly the old CB had been more relaxed under other leader's tutelage (even "genteel" if you like), but all things change.

When I originally accepted a senior position on Jim's team, he was forthright in his expectations of me. He stated that I had the reputation of being a maverick and while he appreciated an independent spirit, he said that on occasion, I would have to swallow hard and accept the direction of the majority. I was obviously naïve; the "majority" rarely turned out to be a group consensus, but invariably a "Jim" solution!

We were all sorely tried at board meetings. A number of the board members were outside directors, and Jim felt strongly that the employee directors should show a united front in their presence. Fair enough, but as we seldom got advance notice of his agenda or even his intentions, we were often caught short. Unless you felt strongly about one of his surprises, you sat on it, as otherwise, you would be the subject of the Didion "glare-down" in concert with barbed put downs, all without an arena to explain your position. You knew he was imminently capable of a subtle portrayal to the outside directors that you were entirely full of shit and had probably just crawled out from under a large and slimy rock. At times, he left you feeling like a whore who had just sold out your principles for corporate unity.

Socially, the man is charming, interesting and intellectually diverse. He has a delightful wife, Gloria, and is certainly well accepted in Pebble Beach where he lives. They entertain often and graciously at their home, and have become quite cosmopolitan from their travel and varied interests. Jim might not always have been so worldly. On one occasion in Amsterdam, Gloria, Shirl and I took the canal tour that Jim had pooh-poohed as "touristy." When we returned to the dock, we realized he had spent the past hour wandering the streets and canal fronts and had discovered Amsterdam's "other side," its famous Red Light District. With an attitude that was a mixture of amazement and pleasure, he gave us a guided tour where he pinpointed Amsterdam's famous sex clubs, a smattering of their cannabis shops where marijuana was legally sold and the bay-windowed house fronts where girls advertised their wares from their sitting rooms.

Jim seemed to lose faith in me during the last few years of my career. This coincided with my acceptance of a role to direct the company's international activity. I had anticipated a diminished importance in my new role as my power base as a line manager was gone, and I was overseeing things rather than people. Admittedly I performed no international miracles (other than building a network in Europe, Asia, Mexico and South America without any funding) but in the grim real estate depression of the 90's, we had very limited budgets for international ventures that didn't offer immediate returns to the bottom line. Jim felt that international travel was a boondoggle and that my philosophy of being in the field, where it was happening, was wasteful. I was increasingly kept in the dark and expressed my dissatisfaction to him. Jim responded by going out and acquiring two fine international companies for over 200 million dollars. He neither consulted me nor even told me until a deal had been struck. While the jury may still be out, his vision might be questioned in this case. The acquired companies haven't proportionally improved corporate profitability, and CB has done a mediocre job of assimilating them. As the company is no more an international player now than they were with their former DTZ alliance, you wonder what they realized from the acquisitions other than a new and confusing name, CB Richard Ellis.

Very often, brilliant and decisive men begin to believe their press clippings. They give their trust to few and hold their decisions to be infallible. In fairness, Jim Didion's leadership at CB posted more pluses than minuses. With a little bit more compassion and belief in others, it could have been so much more.

BILL FORBES "URBANE BUT REAL"

Bill Forbes was my father Ned's best friend. While both splendid men, they couldn't have been more different. Bill was built like a quarter-miler, my father more like a defensive tackle. Bill was strikingly handsome with a prodigious head of hair, my father possessed the Marr presentability but his most notable facial asset was a great smile. Bill dressed like a haberdasher while my Dad dressed as an afterthought. While very social, Bill tended to be reserved, my father outgoing. Bill lived to be 93, my father 46.

Bill and Dad both came from middle class families in south central Los Angeles before it became the city's greatest source of "officer needs assistance" requests. They attended Manual Arts High School and were both student leaders at UCLA, the inexpensive alternative to USC, the private, prestigious university in Los Angeles. A digression: From humble beginnings, UCLA has, at the very least, reached parity with USC in both academics and athletics. Giving USC the benefit of the doubt, excellence in academics and athletics might have been driven by a big state budget at UCLA, but the Bruins' real boon, the location of its campus in Westwood, was the consequence of a land grant from the Janss family. The result was a sparkling new campus in the very desirable Westwood area for UCLA, and a substantial enhancement in the value of their remaining land holdings for the Janss'. Thirty years later, a gift of 1000 acres by the Irvine Company generated like results when Orange County was awarded the University of California Irvine.

Bill was a successful media expert before taking over and reviving the family business, the venerable Southern California Music Company. He had a charming family (although not immune to sadness as they tragically lost their youngest daughter while still in her twenties) and was a success in his business, social and public life. As a Regent for the University of California, he was respected for his quick wit, wonderful personality and principles of fairness, all attributes that were integral to his social and business life as well. Bill was an inveterate golfer, playing the game both left-handed and well. He lived a long, and even better, a healthy life.

After Bill's death in 1999, his daughter Julie asked me to speak at his services in the backyard of their Pasadena home. Prior to my arrival, I decided that my theme would be that were Bill to have been here, his only disappointment would be the knowledge that he had outlived all of his contemporaries. Upon arrival however, I saw that the attendees included the beautiful Holly Balthis, a 92 year-old ex-Rose Queen and at least a half a dozen other nonagenarians. I scrapped my script and decided that Bill would have had a hell of a good time attending his own funeral.

IAN MITCHELL "THE RACIST"

I didn't know Ian Mitchell well. While he was a pleasant person, he was a bigot.

Ian managed and was a part owner of the CB Richard Ellis office in Johannesburg, South Africa, an office whose size, market and opportunities should have made it the most prominent of the four CB offices in Africa. Embarrassingly, it was the least impressive. Johannesburg is the financial and commercial center of Africa's most prosperous country. In 1994, Nelson Mandela and his ANC party won free elections, and the blacks gained political rule of the country. This certainly didn't bring economic control. The ten percent of the population that is white (some 4.5 million people) control most of the prime businesses and industries, but the government has been assimilating blacks into major governmental roles, a direction duplicated by business but at a slower pace. It is said today, that an educated black in a power role suffers the most stressful position in the hierarchy. The whites look at him as a token appointment and, after a brief honeymoon, the blacks denigrate him, as he has produced none of the miracles they expected. Their rate of suicide is purportedly the highest in the nation.

Save Johannesburg, the CB Africa network was integrated. Botswana had black and white co-managers, and a black man, Charles Mataure, very capably led Harare in Zimbabwe. Even Durban in South Africa had a substantial number of blacks in responsible positions. But in Johannesburg, only the receptionist was black.

Ian was of British extraction married to a Boer woman. The Boers or Afrikaans are Dutch descendants who first arrived in South Africa in the 16th century. Those of English descent were generally more liberal than the Boers but Ian seemed to have picked up the idiosyncrasies of her nationality, whose credo in the apartheid days had been "take no prisoners". On a South African vacation, Shirl and I contacted Ian and were asked to join him and his wife, Rita, for dinner. They picked us up at our hotel and took us to a small restaurant in Melville, an upscale neighborhood near their home. On the way to the restaurant, they asked if we would mind swinging by their house as they had heard several gunshots when leaving to pick us up and wanted to be sure their property was secure. While the house was fine, the incident pointed out the omnipresent hazards of living in Johannesburg, one of the most dangerous cities in the world. Unlike the Mitchell's, most of the "haves" in Johannesburg live in compounds or have full-time armed guards, a terrible

PETER MARR

way to have to live. Personal security is a cornerstone of their lives. On another occasion while leaving a dinner house near downtown, Ian warned me that the area was too dangerous to stop at signals and he subsequently ran half a dozen red lights before reaching the safety of the motorway.

Ian's bigotry came to a head at a two-day, all-African meeting I had scheduled in Johannesburg. At this forum, he made the announcement in front of his fellow multi-racial managers that he had no intention of hiring blacks, as they were not capable of doing the work. Without exception, his fellow whites in the room found Ian's position both antiquated and abhorrent. For sure, the man possessed a giant set of balls to go public with such a statement.

I had been letting the Africans run their own meeting, but here I had to interrupt and point out to Ian that the other offices represented in the room seemed to do pretty well having embraced integration while at the same time, his integrated competition in Johannesburg was kicking his ass in the marketplace. I also pointed out that within 12 months, his attitude would bring down his segregated company in a nation run by the blacks. The only question was who would close him down first: the government or his partner, CB Richard Ellis.

Shortly after this meeting, Ian retired, and I am told that the Johannesburg office is now integrated.

SHIRLEY SCHIEBER "AN OFF-THE-WALL LADY"

If you are particularly discerning, you will have noticed that Shirley Schieber is the editor of this effort. Better than that, Shirley writes children's stories, is a poetess, a non-stop conversationalist, teaches "A Course in Miracles" and, to top it off, is a self-proclaimed witch. All of this in spite of (or because of) her Stanford education.

Shirley certainly lives somewhere below the poverty line and has no discernible income that I can make out other than some regular

EPILOGUE

contributions from a generous former husband. Her postage expenses alone (she constantly bombards everyone she knows with sayings, Irish limericks, newspaper articles and poems) has to exceed her Social Security.

Shirley lives in the bowels of an illegal Corona del Mar duplex, a two-room basement hovel that she has labeled the "Mole Hole". It is never dirty, just cluttered with what you would expect from one of the daffier members of the Newport Beach intelligentsia. Books, files, knick-knacks of all kinds, funny hats, scarves and even an occasional papier-mâché gnome are permanent parts of the décor of the "Mole Hole".

We met Shirley when we rented the upstairs flat for a year. Shirley introduced herself as our immediate neighbor and mentioned that she practiced witchcraft. She wasn't, isn't and won't ever be a witch, but she put on a pretty good show. One day she knocked on our back door and upon my opening it, she hurled a cornucopia of straw, sticks and bones on the ground at my feet while mumbling some kind of bizarre incantation. On another occasion, I backed my car out of the garage into the alley where I spied Shirley in my rear view mirror. She was in her nightgown with both arms extended towards me as if giving me a curse. I know she didn't have "the power" as I experienced no recurring headaches, quivering bones or nausea.

Shirley definitely marches to the beat of a different drummer but what an "off the wall" tempo it is.

JIM STANLEY "THE KINDLY SHOWBOAT"

I saw Jim Stanley in action long before I met him. Sometime during the sixties, the Trojan Marching Band was performing at halftime during a USC-UCLA football game at the Los Angeles Coliseum. Suddenly a figure emerged from the stands wearing a very large pair of diapers and a paper Napoleon hat while carrying a wooden sword and straddling a broomstick. Mimicking USC's majestic steed Traveler, this buffoon raced up and down the rows of the marching band before confronting the Trojan

PETER MARR

rooting section where he dramatically reared his broomstick up to the perpendicular. While he received a pelting of rotten fruit and beer from the USC fans, he earned a first-class belly laugh from this mammoth crowd of 100,000 people. Later I learned this was Jim Stanley, one of the true "naughty boys" at UCLA.

Jim played a lot of football at UCLA (he even had a year or two as a student coaching assistant) but he was "temporarily out of school" when he did the John Phillip Sousa bandleader shtick. The university authorities had felt they could do without his presence for a year due to another incident that gave UCLA notoriety they didn't relish. Jim and a nucleus of friends were at the Los Angeles Sports Arena, again for a UCLA-USC contest, this time a basketball game. Jim had been drinking. During the game, he took umbrage to the manner in which a USC star was manhandling his roommate, a Bruin starting guard. Jim suddenly and magically appeared on the court and launched a haymaker at the Trojan guard. It connected flush on his chin. Jim disappeared in the crowd. A full-blown riot broke out where the Trojan coach threw a punch at the high-minded John Wooden, who was to become the most legendary coach in basketball history. This main event was captured on film (but only showing Jim's backside) and Jim received excellent coverage on the wire services. *Sports Illustrated* came out with a photo and caption, "Mystery fan starts riot." He turned himself in to the UCLA authorities the following day.

Jim's shenanigans at school are comical but are not a true indication of the man. While he is a stand-up comic of near professional status, his worth as a man is much deeper than that. His marvelous sense of humor allows him to dominate situations and personally open opportunities to him that otherwise might have gone begging. What he does once he gets there is more important, he makes people happy.

Jim is a tremendous morale builder, an outstanding businessman and a first class husband and father. It feels good to be around him, and he refuses to get down on himself or anyone else. He has recently suffered from a very serious illness. I visited him in Sacramento with some trepidation, for when I called his wife, Susie, she said it best my visit be unannounced. I arrived at a darkened house and thought the worst when no one answered the doorbell. Just as I was rather timidly preparing to ring again, the door flew open and there stood Jim, tubes up his nose, a gaping hole next to his voice box and trailing IV lines. On his head was a huge hat topped with an oversized replica of a cheeseburger, and on his face, the world's biggest grin! What a guy!

HARVEY RANSON "A DIFFERENT BREED"

I only met Harvey Ranson once and maybe his impact on me emanated from the certain trepidation one experiences when visiting his adopted hometown, Bogotá, Colombia. I think not, however. The Ransons were British Jews and moved to Bogotá in a time when it was a much safer place. They located there for its centrality to both Central and South America. They were commercial real estate brokers and advisors who worked the smaller Latin American countries on behalf of multi-national corporations. These companies had experienced the very devil of a time finding qualified local brokerage help for their requirements in say, Guayaquil or Tegucigalpa. Harvey developed a territory that consisted of all the second tier countries of Latin America, countries that couldn't justify their own high quality local specialists.

Harvey and Anna were a good combo. Harvey did the field work and Anna the organization. As they were the "only deal in town", they had lots of business and usually received advances from the multinationals to cover their expenses while finding or confirming a location for them. Harvey was tough, cantankerous and didn't suffer fools well. A great P.R. man he was not, for if crossed, he would tell the company to shove it and fill their own requirement. Maybe a little repugnant, but haven't all of us wished we could do exactly the same when dealing with a very special jerk for a client?

Bogotá seems even more dangerous than Johannesburg but much more beautiful. It sits at the base of a forested flank of the Andes where a funicular slowly climbs its slopes to a spectacularly sited church above the town. The downtown rings of old Spain with leafy avenidas circling its edges. It is sometimes necessary to remind yourself that this is the kidnapping capital of the world as well as home to some of South America's most abject poverty.

Harvey and Anna live and work in a house on the mountain slope above downtown. They have no signs, no advertising and no automobile—they use taxis exclusively as they don't want to draw attention to themselves. A few months before my visit, their 16-year-old son had been kidnapped although they harbored a suspicion that he was part of the kidnapping ring. He was held for several weeks and while their conversations about the incident were still guarded, it appears they paid a ransom (excuse the pun) for his release. Since he had not been a model son and was running with a suspect crowd, they nursed some thoughts that he had been part of the scheme. He must have been a nasty little bastard!

Harvey was a fine host during my short visit to Bogotá in the mid-nineties. We toured the city's famous Gold Museum, shopped in some very nice tiendas near the cathedral, took the cable car to the top of the mountain and wandered through the most successful shopping center in the country. It was very impressive but I wanted more. I told Harvey and the cab driver that I would like to see where the poor people live so I could better understand how the city worked.

When experiencing a new city, I always asked to see where the rich people lived, where the poor people lived, the university, stadium, best shopping areas, industrial parks and anything special about their city that made them proud. The resultant tour gave a sweeping overview of the city, rather important for a simple real estate man. Harvey was tremendously reticent to show their slums, but I kept prodding, and ultimately, Harvey and the driver reluctantly relented. We drove into a

EPILOGUE

nasty area near the cathedral. They locked the cab doors, rolled up the windows and warned me to have no eye contact with anyone outside. Mean, angry-looking men, evil-looking men, hardened looking men as well as clusters of streetwalkers (shockingly, many with small children in tow) lounged at every doorway. Ragamuffin children ran, spit, cursed and kicked at the trashcans that spewed rancid smelling smoke and darting flames on that chilly morning. Hard eyes and mean countenances followed our slow progress through the throngs; we were obviously being sized up as easy prey. The mood of the group left me feeling threatened and frightened. I told Harvey that his point was made; I had seen enough and wouldn't endanger the three of us any longer. He replied, "Thanks," and we left immediately.

The Bogotá visit was timely, as we were able to refer a number of clients to the Ransons. However, the real impression I left with was of the hopelessness of the children, then and in the future. So sad. The Ransons deserve to reap the benefits of their toil in exchange for their valor in voluntarily accepting such a life style.

BRIAN BERTHA "ENERGY PERSONIFIED"

The expression "larger than life" was invented to describe Brian Bertha. Brian lived life to the fullest. Whether he worked or played (proportionally he spent about half his time on each), it was at full speed. His energy had no limits, and his personal esprit pulled many of us with less vigor along for the ride.

California was perfect for Brian. He left his hometown of Chicago, earned a MBA at Berkeley and full of more piss and vinegar than a fish and chips house, he took on the torrid Orange County real estate market. His first boss, John Parker, recognized all of this energy and ego and put Brian to work selling tract homes. Trying to sell tract homes to bored housewives, tire-kickers and interior decorators looking for ideas, communicates humility to even the most vain, and Brian heeded the lesson well. He ultimately became one of the top retail salespeople in the country while only working about half of the time.

Brian never slowed down. At work, he was a whirlwind. He would work a series of 16-hour days, take turnaround trips across the country to solidify a restaurant deal and head home for a few more days of non-stop labor. Then Brian would disappear. He would reappear, usually in Sun Valley, and ski 90 days a year with whomever dared get on a slope with him. His girlfriends often were ski instructors, his male friends were required to ski with the same abandon he did and his two boys, Al and Andy, skied as well as instructors by the time they were ten. Brian had a love affair with a prototype ski, The Ski, which though very fast was quite brittle—at least in Brian's possession. Rad Dye, a friend and the dealer's rep, kept replacing the ones Brian broke, and that usually meant up to 10 mangled pairs of skis a year. Comping that many pairs of skis, it is obvious why the company no longer produces skis. Brian's own destruction derby had to be a factor in their bankruptcy.

Other sports intrigued Brian as well. Surfing, flying, parachuting and mountain climbing—he tried them all. Only hang-gliding failed to pass his muster. He once told me, "That is lunacy—a sure way to kill yourself." That judgment coming from Brian was enough for me. I never gave the sport a try.

Maybe fate felt that Brian had crammed way too much action into the 42 years that he had attacked life. With a friend, Brian was piloting a small plane from Sun Valley to Orange County. They hit a brutal snowstorm over the backcountry of the High Sierra and crashed into the mountains. By all accounts, the weather was too severe for any single engine plane, but after all, we had all felt Brian was immortal. Sadly, in some perverse way, he may have started believing us. Brian has stayed with us. His vital personality was so pervasive that his name comes up with such regularity that you sense that he really never left.

EPILOGUE

C.Y. LEUNG "THE QUIET MOVER AND SHAKER"

I had heard of Chun-ying (C.Y.) Leung well before I met him. He had been the superstar at Jones, Lang Wooten, at the time, the pre-eminent Hong Kong Property Agency. C.Y. was passed by for the managing director's job of their Hong Kong agency when JLW selected an Englishman (well qualified I am sure) for the position. Their timing couldn't have been worse as the People's Republic of China was taking ownership of Hong Kong in 1997 and now, Jones Lang was picking another Brit to lead them through those years, years that they knew had to be difficult ones for the old guard. I thought it just might have been isolated stupidity, but JLW did the same thing in Singapore with its top man there, Edmund Tie. The end result was both men walked out with JLW's best Asian employees, formed their own companies and made enormous inroads into the production of their former employer.

I had a series of trips to Hong Kong for meetings with C.Y. along with Derek Butler, my DTZ counterpart and our old associate, Greg Spinner. We were negotiating an agreement for the Asian connection that Derek's and my companies both badly needed if we were to offer our clients true international coverage. In the short term, we were successful. Long term, C.Y has to wonder, how did I ever get involved with those damned Americans.

C.Y. was tall, good looking and with a charming presence, he bridged the gap between east and west better than anyone I had ever seen. He was entirely at home at a western social event or business function and could "small talk" on most anything you might want to chat about. Most of all, he was Chinese. When CB Chairman Jim Didion got crossways with C.Y., he commented privately that the man was "a god damn communist." C.Y. was no communist as he always displayed an abiding faith in capitalism. However (and certainly understandably), he did have a deep love and high hopes for China. Very early in his career, he opened up communication lines within the People's Republic of China. He chose his contacts well. He became a real estate advisor to Zhu Rongii, then Mayor of Shanghai and later Premier of the People's Republic. Possibly, in part due to these contacts, C.Y. is now Convenor on the Hong Kong Executive Council and I am told is one of the two or three most important people in the former colony. Enough said.

C.Y. also became an advocate for Li Ka Shing in China. Li, one of the world's richest and most powerful men, had committed to Oriental Plaza in central Beijing and built a project (at the expense of China's first McDonalds which was demolished) that is considered the heart of the new market-driven China. In 1996, Li Ka Shing's son, Victor, was kidnapped by a notorious mainland gangster Cheung Tze-keung (with the colorful alias of "Big Spender") and later released upon payment of a ransom reported to have been $100 million U.S. The kidnapper fled back to China. Purportedly, Li used a couple of his chits in Beijing, for the People's Republic quickly seized, tried and executed "Big Spender."

Although our respective firms separated with consequent litigious actions, C.Y. and I have stayed friends. Chairman Jim Didion unilaterally cancelled our alliance, although in fairness not necessarily without good reason. Our cancellation had to be a mortifying blow to C.Y., and it was delivered without an escape hatch for him to save face. Saving face is not an Asian thing; it holds for all of us, and shame on us for having forgotten that.

My friendship with C.Y. flourished in spite of our first business meal at Repulse Bay, on the backside of Hong Kong Island. My agility with chopsticks is suspect, but on this particular day I felt confident about my prowess and reached to the center of the table to remove a plump piece of dim sum. I lost it half way to my month dropping it into the soup where it exploded like a depth charge over my dining partners and me. C.Y. had to think that this potential "gwai lo" partner is a klutz as well.

ZELDA LITTLEFIELD "THE MORMON INFLUENCE"

Zelda Hardy Boone Johnson Littlefield is my mother-in-law. She is a practicing Mormon or more formally, a member of the Church of the

EPILOGUE

Latter Day Saints. When I first met Zelda, I liked to puff a pipe and take an occasional cocktail. As a result, I was not initially her ideal future son-in-law. However, Zelda knows not to take everything at face value (fortunately for me) and now we belong to a mutual admiration society—at least, I think we do!

Mormons have always been a major force in Utah but few realize that they simultaneously became politically and economically powerful in many parts of Arizona, Nevada, Wyoming and Idaho. Such diverse communities as Pocatello, Idaho (which has 23 places of LDS worship today) or Las Vegas, Nevada (which the Mormons first settled in 1855) have been heavily influenced by the Mormon culture.

Zelda was the seventh of sixteen children born to Warren and Laura Hardy of Tucson. The family was extremely close knit (pretty much of a given with Mormon families) which was a salvation when Zelda's brothers, George and Ellis, were both lost on Iwo Jima.

Zelda's grandparents had migrated to the deserts of northern Mexico in the latter part of the 19th century. They and others had moved to Mexico to keep their families and lifestyles intact after the banning of polygamy in the states. They settled in the Casasgrandes area in the state of Chihuahua. Zelda's father Warren was born in Mexico, and he had three wives there with Zelda's mother Laura being the first. He also took two wives whose husbands had been killed. He ultimately was responsible for a total of 36 children. The Church of Latter Day Saints had abandoned the practice of polygamy at the turn of the century, but plural marriages (whether they were condoned by the church or not is still debated) existed in Mexico.

The choices for polygamous mates were dictated by the local church leaders and were spiritually and economically inspired rather than sensually motivated. Often successful men were asked to marry widows or impoverished women of the faith. It couldn't have all been idyllic. Grandfather Hardy once told my wife Shirl, "I have spent many a night in that hay barn more than I ever spent with those women". With 36 children, Grandfather Hardy may have been guilty of mild exaggeration!

In 1916, with Pancho Villa terrorizing northern Mexico, the Hardys felt that living polygamy in the states outweighed the risk of dodging banditos in Mexico, and Warren dispatched a pregnant Laura and five children to Salt Lake while he stayed in Mexico to defend the homestead. Laura never reached Salt Lake instead settling into an abandoned house in Tucson. The intensity of Pancho Villa's onslaught forced Warren to follow Laura north but it took lots of time and anguish before he learned she was in Tucson, some 800 miles from where he expected to find her. Talk about pioneer stock being tough!

Zelda is now the matriarch of the Hardy clan, which numbers over 300 strong. Every year they meet for a three-day campout on the White River near Fort Apache in the eastern mountains of Arizona. It is perhaps fitting that such a significant family of the west meet in such historical grounds.

COR VAN ZADELHOFF "THE SELF-MADE MAN"

Cornelius Van Zadelhoff is a Dutchman (and a very flamboyant one at that) who built and ran one of Europe's most successful real estate operations. Cor, an extremely imposing man, (he is at least six and a half feet tall) has a most pandemic variety of interests, both business and personal. He is, a traditionalist (he has acquired the Dutch equivalent of historic monuments for many of his branch offices), promoter (he owns a fleet of balloons, emblazoned with his logo, that he constantly floats across the country,) clever businessman (balloons and historic monuments have wonderful tax advantages) and a man of civic responsibility. Without pay, he took over the leadership of the successful construction of the 60,000 seat indoor Amsterdam Arena when it was floundering.

One of Cor's early feats was to build a commercial property company that covered all corners of Holland, from Rotterdam to Utrecht. With his promotional skills and handsome demeanor, he soon became a highly

EPILOGUE

recognizable personality throughout Holland, Van Zadelhoff, the "Z" of DTZ (Debenham Thorpe Zadelhoff), couldn't persuade his more conservative British partners to open offices in economically risky Eastern Europe, so he funded the offices personally thus completing a network of DTZ offices from Budapest to Moscow. In return, he received a first look at any property these offices might generate. Dumb like a vos, no?

Cor was the son of a horse trader from the little town of Bruekelen (from whence the Flatbush borough in New York got its name) south of Amsterdam. Several years ago I was an overnight guest of Cor and Janet on their 80 acre spread which fronts on the canal that bisects Bruekelen. Now if 80 acres is impressive in the US, it is overwhelming in Holland. Cor and Janet have taken an old farm house, converted it with great taste and added a barn to house his collection of antique wagons (it costs him nothing as he has made them available to the Dutch government in exchange for the government underwriting his maintenance expense). They also have added a menagerie of hoofed animals and a polo field where, even though he doesn't ride, he throws an annual polo soiree just to enjoy a good party.

While Cor and Janet are childless, he has six siblings with whom he is very close. I am told that after Cor became successful, he offered to underwrite individual annual vacations for all of the members of his family. The first year the requests were modest, perhaps for trips to the Isle of Sylt or Bruges. Now he practically needs to own a travel agency (perhaps he does) as they go to the Seychelles, Little Dix Bay, Aspen and Bali. I am told that this is just what Cor wanted, and it makes him happy to see them sharing in his success. Nice move!

Cor is the life of the party, a man of fun who people enjoy being with. He didn't gain his great success by being a pushover and Cor is definitely someone you want on your side.

PETER MARR

Bill May "Mr. Nice Guy"

Shirl and I met Bill May when he was 84. Bill and his wife Kathleen had joined a group of us hiking through the challenging hills of Capri and the Amalfi Drive in the south of Italy. Bill, a tall and solid man, was 20 years older than any of his fellow hikers and outlasted most them. Kathleen had a definite spark, an effervescent spirit and clearly was behind much that this remarkable man had accomplished.

Bill started his business career as an engineer at Dupont before moving to American Can where ultimately, he became Chief Executive Officer. After retiring, he became Dean of the Business School at N.Y.U. before accepting the responsibility of rebuilding the Statue of Liberty and Ellis Island where, for the past ten years, he has served as president for the magnanimous sum of a dollar a year.

During his career, he met most of the American presidents and an impressive number of national leaders, celebrated athletes and "captains of industry". He certainly has enough renowned acquaintances to qualify as a potential world-class namedropper, but he finds this abhorrent. A group of us were chatting one evening about Slobodan Milosevic, the thug who was formerly the Serbian president. Bill mentioned that he had met with the man once and found him to be totally reprehensible. We asked how that had come about and he said that when he was a director of Salomon Brothers, he had been asked to head a committee to explore a major loan to the Yugoslavs. Another time, we asked him how he managed to stay in such good shape. It was only then that he admitted he had just won the Senior Olympics in the discus. God only knows what you might learn about him if you made an effort.

Bill is unaffected, natural and friendly. Our time together was brief, his impact was lasting.

EPILOGUE

JOAQUIN AYALA "THE DROLL WIT"

Joaquin managed the Club de Caza y Pesca Las Cruces, which translates to the Club of Hunting and Fishing of the Crosses. Las Cruces is near the southern tip of Baja California about an hour from its biggest city, La Paz. Access is either by fairly primitive roads or for those members with a personal aircraft in their arsenal, a 2500' landing strip. For years, the owners have turned down government offers to improve the road. They know its isolation is one of its greatest assets.

In 1948, Abelardo Rodriguez, a former president of Mexico, added a ranch of over 10,000 acres to his already substantial holdings in Baja. It included five and a half miles of pristine shoreline. A legendary holding discovered by Hernan Cortez, it had been the source of countless pearls but the oysters were obliterated in 1929 by a mysterious disease. All that remained were a couple of thatched huts and the remnants of old aqueducts and tropical gardens. Rodriguez, in partnership with several Americans (including Bing Crosby and Desi Arnaz), revived this treasure and built the private club that thrives there today. The Rodriguez family was bright enough to see that Joaquin became the "hired gun" to run the club and grandson Nicky provided the "arms length" ownership attention.

Joaquin was a slender, droll man who took to Mexican cowboy attire and who knew everything that happened at Las Cruces, La Paz and presumably the entire peninsula of Baja. If you needed something (anything from a ponga to presumably a puta), Joaquin would find it for you. If you were one of the "less fortunate" souls, as we were, and were flying into La Paz commercially rather than on your own plane, Joaquin was there at the La Paz Airport to meet you. At the airport, everything was greased from customs to porters, and once you were ensconced in the Suburban, you just asked Joaquin, "Who do I owe what?" Leaving the porters with big-league happy faces, he would then jump into the Suburban and at breakneck speeds for the washboard roads, navigate the cacti, the arroyos and the hill tops with their "knock you dead" seashore vistas that acclimated you for your arrival at the idyllic Las Cruces.

Joaquin had to be a great manager as he kept a top-notch staff together for several decades. Chacho and Jesus in the bar, Consuela and Maria in the kitchen and a multitude of others (maids, gardeners fishermen, and maintenance men—mostly incognito to the guests) had received their 30-year pins. As a result, whenever you returned to Las Cruces, you felt you were returning to family. Joaquin could make light of this however. Once, during a busy time at Las Cruces, he was asked, "How many people do you have working here, Joaquin?" He dragged on his ever-lit cigarette, sipped at his tequila, a shot glass of which could generally be found on his presence, and responded, "Well Señor, about half of them!"

Joaquin died a legend in 2001. Those of us who belong to the club just hope that Las Cruces is less affected by his departure than we are.

BILL DOBYNS "COUNTRY BOY"

Bill is a mountain man. He lives on 10 acres on the south slope of a hogback ridge in the Mother Lode country of the Sierra foothills a half hour above Placerville. He is super skinny (totally without a butt), and his 20 cats far outnumber his teeth. He smokes Black Cavendish in a pipe worn down around the edges with two larges gullies eroded into its sides. He always wears a baseball cap with Willies Welding or Peterbilt or some such inscription on it. He is a tough old bird. His wife Vivian (who, not unpleasantly, punctuates all conversation with "Oh Boy!") tells the story of Bill, who after surgery, tired of his catheter and personally removed it. Bill said it felt like a fishing line coming out; something you might catch a shark on.

Bill is my wife Shirl's half-brother who she didn't know existed until two to three years ago. Luther Boone (Shirley and Bill's father, Luther Boone, was somewhat of a rascal and definitely a womanizer) fathered Bill shortly before marrying Shirley's long-suffering mother, Zelda. Bill states, that based on his sexual shenanigans, Luther must be related to Bill Clinton. Being naturally curious about his real origins, and with some fine

EPILOGUE

detective work, Bill traced down Luther's bloodline and made contact with Shirl and her brother, Jim. After many telephone conversations, Shirl and Jim decided they had to meet their brother. As we drove to his ranch in the summer of 2001, we all tried to guess just how Bill Dobyns might look. We conjured up an image of a man with a full head of hair, a beer belly and a marvelous set of teeth. Our assumptions were faulty, but he does have a fine head of hair.

Bill loves his animals. On his ten acres, he has the aforementioned cats, two dogs, six horses, one ass, nine chickens, thirty sheep and an irregular cadre of visitors including deer, coyotes, raccoons and cougars. Unlike many remote rural properties, his yard harbors no abandoned iceboxes, old tools or wagons, but he does have a passion for motorized vehicles. Splayed around its perimeter are a panel truck, a 1953 Ferguson tractor, a vintage '60s Ford Fairlane, a '23 Ford ice truck, a Starcraft trailer and a '79 Jimmy diesel which Bill swears can do 80 towing his Starcraft up the Altamont grade.

The closest neighbors down the hill from him, the Limas, are weekenders. They are large people and Bill refers to them as "wide bodies." When they turn on the lights when they arrive, Bill says, "The airport is open".

I have only met him that once, but know I will need another "Bill Dobyns fix" before long. Bill is a true frontiersman, but best of all, a bona-fide life-sized character.

Altogether, I have been inspired and intrigued by these various versatile people, and have learned a little bit more about life from each of them. I thank them for the opportunity to add them to "Dust on my Shoulders".